Mary-Kate and Ashley Olsen

by Terri Dougherty

LUCENT BOOKS

An imprint of Thomson Gale, a part of The Thomson Corporation

Detroit • New York • San Francisco • San Diego • New Haven, Conn.
Waterville, Maine • London • Munich

For more information, contact
Lucent Books
27500 Drake Rd.
Farmington Hills, MI 48331-3535
Or you can visit our Internet site at http://www.gale.com

LIBRARY OF CONGRESS CATALOGING-IN-PUBLICATION DATA

Dougherty, Terri.
  Mary-Kate and Ashley Olsen / by Terri Dougherty.
    p. cm. — (People in the news)
  Includes bibliographical references and index.
  ISBN 1-59018-720-2 (alk. paper)
  1. Olsen, Mary-Kate, 1986– —Juvenile literature. 2. Olsen, Ashley, 1986– —Juvenile literature. 3. Actors—United States—Biography—Juvenile literature. I. Title. II. Series: People in the news (San Diego, Calif.)
  PN2287.O36D68 2005
  792.02'8'092273—dc22
                                                                    2004023199

Printed in the United States of America

Table of Contents

Foreword

FAME AND CELEBRITY are alluring. People are drawn to those who walk in fame's spotlight, whether they are known for great accomplishments or for notorious deeds. The lives of the famous pique public interest and attract attention, perhaps because their experiences seem in some ways so different from, yet in other ways so similar to, our own.

Newspapers, magazines, and television regularly capitalize on this fascination with celebrity by running profiles of famous people. For example, television programs such as *Entertainment Tonight* devote all of their programming to stories about entertainment and entertainers. Magazines such as *People* fill their pages with stories of the private lives of famous people. Even newspapers, newsmagazines, and television news frequently delve into the lives of well-known personalities. Despite the number of articles and programs, few provide more than a superficial glimpse at their subjects.

Lucent's People in the News series offers young readers a deeper look into the lives of today's news makers, the influences that have shaped them, and the impact they have had in their fields of endeavor and on other people's lives. The subjects of the series hail from many disciplines and walks of life. They include authors, musicians, athletes, political leaders, entertainers, entrepreneurs, and others who have made a mark on modern life and who, in many cases, will continue to do so for years to come.

These biographies are more than factual chronicles. Each book emphasizes the contributions, accomplishments, or deeds that have brought fame or notoriety to the individual and shows how that person has influenced modern life. Authors portray their subjects in a realistic, unsentimental light. For example, Bill Gates—the cofounder and chief executive officer of the software giant Microsoft—has been instrumental in making personal computers the most vital tool of the modern age. Few dispute his business savvy, his perseverance, or his technical expertise, yet critics say he is ruthless in his dealings with competitors and driven more by his desire to maintain Microsoft's dominance in the computer industry than by an interest in furthering technology.

In these books, young readers will encounter inspiring stories about real people who achieved success despite enormous obstacles. Oprah Winfrey—the most powerful, most watched, and wealthiest woman on television today—spent the first six years of her life in the care of her grandparents while her unwed mother sought work and a better life elsewhere. Her adolescence was colored by promiscuity, pregnancy at age fourteen, rape, and sexual abuse.

Each author documents and supports his or her work with an array of primary and secondary source quotations taken from diaries, letters, speeches, and interviews. All quotes are footnoted to show readers exactly how and where biographers derive their information and provide guidance for further research. The quotations enliven the text by giving readers eyewitness views of the life and accomplishments of each person covered in the People in the News series.

In addition, each book in the series includes photographs, annotated bibliographies, timelines, and comprehensive indexes. For both the casual reader and the student researcher, the People in the News series offers insight into the lives of today's news makers—people who shape the way we live, work, and play in the modern age.

Introduction

Living an Image

MARY-KATE AND ASHLEY Olsen have grown up in front of the camera. Just babies when they made their first appearance on television's *Full House,* they have gone from chubby-cheeked, goggle-eyed toddlers to spunky adolescents to blossoming teenagers before the eyes of American TV audiences. From their first shaky steps to their excitement over getting driver's licenses, many people have witnessed their progression on film.

When Mary-Kate and Ashley were young, their cute antics endeared them to fans. As they grew older, their wholesome, adventurous image made them role models for young girls. Their movies, videos, and books let girls imagine that they, too, could be detectives, singers, and leaders among their friends. Through their on-screen personas, Mary-Kate and Ashley shared family vacations, dilemmas about boys, and adventures in London, Rome, and Paris.

Mary-Kate and Ashley cultivated a clean, charming image, and it was this image rather than their acting talent that endeared them to fans and extended their appeal well beyond television. The girls also lent their names to a line of clothing, perfume, jewelry and other products geared toward young girls. Under the guidance of savvy entertainment lawyer Robert Thorne, they have parlayed their wholesome image into a billion-dollar business. They have used their own likes and dislikes to hone a brand of products targeted at young girls that reflects their tastes and the values they represent.

Promoting so many products with their names on them meant the girls were also under pressure to live up to the image they had created. Their products represented what girls aspired to become and what parents wanted their daughters to be: fun-loving yet rule-following, popular and kind, cheerful and wholesome. To a point, they handled this enormous responsibility extremely well. Although they could certainly afford to lead lives of glitz and glamour, the Olsens managed to stay grounded through their high school years, and they did not spend extravagantly or rebel wildly. They seemed to have avoided the pitfalls that can come with having a great deal of money at a young age. While a trust fund protected their millions of dollars, they protected their image by appearing to stay away from drinking and drugs.

They were not, however, immune to pressure from their friends and themselves. As they entered their later years of high school, they were photographed at drinking parties and began to feel the pressure of living up to an unattainably perfect image. A hectic schedule, the glare of the media spotlight, and stress over precollege exams contributed to Mary-Kate's developing an eating disorder. She is recovering with support from her sister, but it is unlikely that her life will get less stressful any time soon.

Throughout their career, the Olsen twins have portrayed a very wholesome image. Here, Mary-Kate and Ashley pose on the set of the 1999 television movie Switching Goals.

Now in their late teens, the Olsen twins face the challenge of transitioning from child stars to adult actresses.

Mary-Kate and Ashley face new challenges as they near adulthood and must make decisions about which direction to take their lives as they try to make the transition from child stars to having adult careers. They are enjoying the freedom that comes with adulthood, but are also bound to the work that comes with holding up an entertainment empire that has been growing up around them since they were toddlers.

Chapter 1

Little Stars

On Friday, June 13, 1986, Jarnette and David Olsen became the proud parents of twin girls when their daughters Mary-Kate and Ashley were born. Ashley Fuller Olsen was born first, coming into the world two minutes before her sister. Ashley was given her mom's maiden name as her middle name, while Mary-Kate was given a dual first name, but no middle name. The fraternal twins were not the only children in their family. Their older brother, Trent, was born in 1984. The girls would become big sisters at three years old when Elizabeth, or Lizzie, was born in 1989.

By the time Lizzie was born, the twins were not just big sisters, they were on their way to becoming big stars. They would be in the show business spotlight before they blew out the candle on their first birthday cake. Their babyhood would be shared with a television audience, and some of their preschool fun would include acting in front of a camera. Their popularity meant that their parents had to take on another role in addition to caring for their young daughters: They would have to think about how to best guide their careers.

The Audition

Show business was not something that ran in the Olsen family. They lived in Sherman Oaks, California, a community in the San Fernando Valley, not far from the movie studios of Hollywood. Though they lived near Hollywood, neither Jarnette nor David had a job inside the entertainment industry. Jarnette, who was called Jarnie, was a former professional ballet dancer who stayed home to care for the children, and David was a mortgage broker. They had no acting aspirations for Mary-Kate and Ashley or their other children—until a chance meeting changed everything.

When the twins were a few months old, Jarnette went shopping with a friend. The friend had a child who was interested in acting, and the women stopped at the office of the child's agent. After Jarnette commented that she had twin daughters, the agent asked her to send in some photos. Not thinking anything would come of it, Jarnette sent a snapshot to the talent agency. To Jarnette's surprise, the photo landed the twins an audition for a new television show about a family that included a baby girl.

The producers wanted to cast twins in the role of the baby because child labor laws restricted the amount of time young children were allowed to work. Because babies between six months and two years of age could work for only two hours each day,

In 2004 Mary-Kate and Ashley pose with their family after receiving a star on Hollywood's Walk of Fame. The twins have been acting since infancy.

The San Fernando Valley

Mary-Kate and Ashley Olsen grew up in the San Fernando Valley, an urban area in Southern California nestled among several mountain ranges. Most of the communities in the valley are part of the city of Los Angeles, although several other cities, such as Burbank and Hidden Hills, are located in the valley as well.

The twins were born in the valley community of Sherman Oaks. The city is mainly a bedroom community, and most of the people who live there commute to another city to work. While family businesses line Ventura Boulevard, its main street, the community became a cultural icon in the 1980s because of its main shopping center, the Sherman Oaks Galleria. Frank Zappa's song "Valley Girl," sung by his daughter Moon Unit, and a movie of the same name caricaturized the speech patterns, shopping habits, and empty-headedness of the teens who frequented the Galleria's stores. Besides the Olsen twins, celebrities who have lived in Sherman Oaks include Marilyn Monroe, Liberace, Stan Laurel, and Oliver Hardy.

using twins would give the show's producers twice the amount of time to put a baby in front of the camera and twice as many chances to get the scene right. Even though they were chosen to audition, Jarnette still did not think it was the beginning of a career for the girls. "I just thought it might be fun," she said. "It was a way to get out of the house and do something a little out of the ordinary."[1]

When they were about six months old, the Olsen twins went on their first and only audition. They waited in the reception area with six other sets of twins, who were getting crabbier by the minute. Mary-Kate and Ashley did not seem to be fazed by their new surroundings or the cries of the other babies, however. When it was their turn to audition, the show's producers were impressed with how happy the girls were. Even though another set of twins had already been penciled in for the part, Mary-Kate and Ashley's engaging eyes, attentiveness, and easygoing dispositions quickly won over the producers. "Ashley and Mary-Kate had a great time," said Jeff Franklin, the series's creator and executive producer. "They were happy kids with these amazing big blue eyes."[2] The little girls did not realize what was going on at the time, but they had just charmed their way into the role of Michelle in the television sitcom *Full House,* a move that would be the beginning of a career that would take them from a being a cute pair of babies to a couple of superstars.

Working Babies

At nine months old Mary-Kate and Ashley went to work on the pilot—a sample show of a proposed television series. Soon after, the show was picked up by ABC, and together the twins earned $2,400 per episode. In September 1987 they were introduced to television viewers when actor John Stamos, playing their character's Uncle Jesse, carried Michelle onstage. The first few shows featured Mary-Kate more than Ashley, as Ashley had a tendency to cry when placed in front of the camera. However, when Mary-Kate got a sore eye and could not perform, Ashley was featured more often.

The producers of *Full House* did not emphasize the fact that Michelle was played by twins. The credits for the pilot list the character of Michelle as played by "Mary Kate Ashley Olsen." It was difficult to tell the babies apart; they looked so much alike that even their parents relied on a freckle to tell who was who.

Calling It Quits?

While Mary-Kate and Ashley continued to be happy babies who seemed to enjoy being on the set, their acting careers almost ended after their first season on *Full House*. Their job was difficult for their parents, who had to manage their own lives and those of the rest of the family, as well as get their daughters to work and make sure they were happy and well cared-for there. Their family was not used to working around the demands of a television series, and David and Jarnette considered taking the girls off the show after the first season.

David and Jarnette did not want acting to become a burden for the girls or for the rest of the family. When the girls were at work, one or both parents were always with them. This meant that David and Jarnette had to change their schedules to accommodate the girls' work. However, it also allowed them to see that the girls clearly liked being at the studio. As long as they enjoyed what they were doing, their parents decided to let them continue in the role.

The fact that Mary-Kate and Ashley were fraternal rather than identical twins also almost cost them the role of Michelle as they grew from babies to toddlers. The part of a baby on a television show is sometimes recast as the child grows older or one twin is chosen to take over the part. Although Mary-Kate and Ashley look very much alike, as fraternal twins there was a chance that

This photo shows Ashley as a toddler. The twins' cute faces and happy demeanor helped them land the role of Michelle on the television sitcom Full House.

as they grew older they would become more dissimilar in appearance. If their looks changed too much, audiences would be able to tell them apart, which would not work on a show in which they tag-teamed as a single character. Luckily, they continued to look so much alike that audiences could not tell the difference.

Many viewers soon realized, however, that Michelle was played by twins. By the end of the first season, both of their names were appearing in the show's credits. In one show, they both appeared on screen at the same time: When the freewheeling Uncle Jesse is feeling overwhelmed by all the kids around him, both twins are in a scene that emphasizes his fear that the kids are taking over his life. Since it was clear that Michelle was played by two babies, producers feared a backlash from fans if they chose one twin over the other. Not wanting to hurt the show's popularity, the producers let Mary-Kate and Ashley continue to share the role of Michelle.

Capturing an Audience

The expressive eyes that had gotten the Olsens the role as Michelle also endeared the character to viewers. *Full House* was initially criticized for its lame jokes and thin plotlines. Although early reviews of the show were not complimentary, the twins and the show eventually won over a loyal audience. By its third season *Full House* regularly appeared in the top twenty shows of the week, and it later climbed into the top ten, largely due to the appeal of its youngest stars. The audience loved watching the character Michelle grow up, reaching milestones such as moving out of the crib, learning to talk, and taking her first steps.

The twins each had different strengths that allowed baby Michelle to display a well-rounded personality. Ashley took over the more sensitive scenes and, when the twins began to talk, had the more serious lines. Mary-Kate showed a sassier and brasher side of Michelle's personality and later did the more action-oriented and emotional scenes. The girls' complementary personalities gave the show's producers plenty of material to work with and allowed them to feature Michelle in a variety of situations. She did everything from learning to skip to strutting across the stage with attitude.

Full House

Full House, the series that launched the Olsen twins' acting careers, was a family-oriented sitcom that was part of ABC's Friday night lineup. The show featured Bob Saget as Danny Tanner, a widower raising his three young daughters. He was helped by his best friend, aspiring comedian Joey Gladstone (Dave Coulier), and brother-in-law, Jesse Katsopolis (John Stamos). While the Olsens paired up to play Michelle, the youngest Tanner, Jodie Sweetin played their sister Stephanie, and Candace Cameron had the part of D.J., the oldest of the Tanner children.

While Saget played the reliable father figure who was always there for his girls and anyone else who needed him, his character was also befuddled enough to admit that he needed help with and from the girls. His friend Joey was childlike enough to identify with the kids and make them laugh. Uncle Jesse was a cool musician, who was tender and caring despite his tough image.

The show's plots revolved around the three men trying to help the girls navigate through childhood by helping them make it through tough times such as the first day of school, a case of the chicken pox, and a bad grade in Spanish class. It also got laughs from the three men running the household, from dad Danny's incessant cleaning to Joey and Jesse making a mess changing Michelle's diaper. Jesse's yearning for his days of independence was also at the center of many episodes, and his romance and marriage to Rebecca Donaldson (Lori Loughlin) became a major story line on the show.

The show premiered on September 22, 1987. It ran for 192 episodes, with its last show airing on August 29, 1995. The series is still shown heavily in reruns and is often seen on Nickelodeon.

Ashley poses with the cast of Full House. *The popular show ran a full eight seasons.*

Patient Preschoolers

Part of the reason for the twins' success as young actresses was that even though they were only preschoolers, Mary-Kate and Ashley were very open to taking direction. When they were very young, a cookie would be held off camera to make them smile or giggle. As they grew from toddlers to preschoolers, acting coach Adria Later would act out the scenes and have them mimic her, and then give them cues as they performed before the cameras. The twins would repeat what she said, and her voice would later be edited out of the scene.

Mary-Kate and Ashley viewed acting as a game of follow the leader, and would happily walk, talk, or grimace the way their

Ashley performs a scene with Full House *costar John Stamos. The twins' ability to follow directions made them terrific child actresses.*

teacher asked them to. Soon they were memorizing some of their lines and had a thumbs-up catchphrase—"You got it, dude"—and another, "No way, José," for when they were showing their independence. Their wide-eyed expressions and deadpan delivery were a hit with audiences, and Michelle was often featured in the show's opening scene as she learned "Ring Around the Rosie," blew bubbles, or played hide and seek. Michelle also became the focus of more episodes, as she was cheered up when missing her friend or taught not to be selfish.

There were occasional power struggles between the show's director and the young stars. When Mary-Kate was about two or three, she realized that if she refused to do something there was not much the adults around her could do about it. In one scene, she was supposed to have peanut butter on her hands. She hated having the squishy peanut butter between her fingers and declared that she wanted it wiped off her hands. She threatened to sing if she had to keep the peanut butter on her hands, and she proceeded to do just that.

The twins had learned that they could control a scene, but fusses like the peanut butter incident were rare. Their patience and willingness to do as they were asked allowed producers to expand their role and play to an audience who loved the girls. Getting a scene right often took multiple tries, but the girls' easygoing nature gave them the stamina they needed to repeat the scene over and over until they got it right. Four-year-old Mary-Kate let the series's dog, Comet, lick her face over and over, while Ashley agreeably took a skipping lesson six times. "We can tell them what's going on in a scene, and we make it a game for them," Franklin said. "They're amazing little troopers."[3]

Just Playing Around

Although they spent some long days at the studio, the girls did not mind going there. Heading to the set was simply part of their lives, just as preschool was. They were at the studio three days a week for three weeks out of the month. They rehearsed on Tuesday, taped on Wednesday, and did the final taping on Thursday. When they were not needed onstage, they retired to a kid-friendly playroom where they could do art projects, play with

Comet, watch classic musical videos, or let their imaginations roam with a variety of toys.

Camaraderie among cast members helped make days at the studio fun for the girls. When actor Bob Saget, who played their dad on the show, could not tell them apart, they would show mock indignation with a hands-on-hips gesture. Dave Coulier, who played Michelle's father's friend Joey Gladstone, enjoyed teasing the girls. When they were about two or three, he told them that they could fly if they ran around and flapped their arms. As they chased him around the studio, he encouraged them to say "tweet, tweet." Silly games such as this with others on the set made acting a game for the youngsters.

The twins went to preschool on weekdays when they were not needed on the set. They also found time to go to the park, have ice cream with their friends, and swim at costar John Stamos's home. Despite all the attention they received on the set and the scenes they were asked to do again and again, they remained normal, imaginative preschoolers. Asked about their future, Mary-Kate said she would like to grow up to be Batgirl, while Ashley had her sights set on being a pom-pom girl.

The twins had begun acting at such a young age that the television studio was just another place for them to play. The girls did not think being on television was anything special. Acting was something they enjoyed, although not because it made them well known. "I like it because I have a dressing room and play school," Ashley said, as Mary-Kate nodded in agreement. [4]

Recognizable Stars

Mary-Kate and Ashley may not have comprehended their success, but by the time they were four years old they had become the star of the show. It was Michelle's face that viewers saw first in the opening credits, and they had the highest TV Q rating (a measure of a star's popularity) of any performer on television. Their popularity outshone even that of veteran stars such as Bill Cosby.

This had some unpleasant consequences for the twins and their family, as they were often recognized when they went out

The Men of *Full House*

Bob Saget played Danny Tanner, a widowed father of three, on *Full House*. Before joining *Full House*, the Philadelphia native was the host of the *Morning Program* on CBS. He graduated from Temple University's film school and was a stand-up comedian before starting his television career. Saget also hosted *America's Funniest Home Videos* while *Full House* was on the air. Saget is also a writer; he wrote several scripts for *America's Funniest Home Videos*.

Dave Coulier did not stray too far from real life with his portrayal of comedian Joey Gladstone on *Full House*. Born in Detroit, Michigan, he was a stand-up comedian who did voices for animated series such as *Muppet Babies* and *The Real Ghostbusters*. He was also the host of *America's Funniest People* between 1990 and 1994, and he appeared on *My Life Is a Sitcom* in 2003.

John Stamos, who played the girls' Uncle Jesse on the series, is a native of Los Angeles who began his work in television on the soap opera *General Hospital* in 1982. He appeared in television movies, often going against his nice-guy character on *Full House* by playing a villain, and he has also appeared onstage in plays such as *Nine* and *How to Succeed in Business Without Really Trying*. He married model and actress Rebecca Romijin in 1998 and invited the Olsen twins and others from the *Full House* cast to the wedding. He and Romijn were divorced in 2004.

Mary-Kate poses with the men of Full House: *(from left) Dave Coulier, John Stamos, and Bob Saget.*

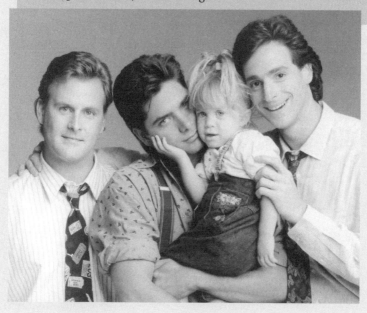

in public. At times the attention was too much. After noticing the twin stars, fans sometimes pulled the family aside and asked to take a photo with the girls. Sometimes so many people approached them that it was frightening for the family.

Being bothered by mobs of fans was something the Olsens had never envisioned when Jarnette sent the twins' snapshot to a talent agent. They had not planned for their daughters to become actresses, much less stars. They were aware that it could end abruptly if the show went off the air, and if that happened their father said it would not bother the family at all. "I would not push acting," he said. "I am more concerned with the girls' education."[5]

For the time being, however, there was no doubt about how the public felt about his daughters, who were the most successful child stars since Shirley Temple. David and Jarnette Olsen realized that their lives were changing as their daughters' popularity increased, and they needed to establish a plan for the girls' futures. Mary-Kate and Ashley were too busy playing and being preschoolers to realize what their stardom meant, but their parents had to decide how to best handle their daughters' growing popularity.

Chapter 2

Building on Stardom

THE OLSENS REALIZED their daughters were talented, but were not certain as parents that they were doing enough to guide the girls' careers. On *Full House* the twins had shown that they had the ability to steal a scene and carry a show. However, their popularity rating showed that they had the potential to do much more than share a role on a television show. Their parents had to decide how to help the girls use their talent and star power to the best of their abilities. By capitalizing on their popularity, the twins eventually branched out into music, books, and videos.

Thorne Steps In

As relative newcomers to the entertainment industry, David and Jarnette knew they were not savvy enough to manage their daughters' careers. They were not familiar with salary negotiations or contracts and had been using an agent to take care of those matters for the girls. However, when others pointed out that the twins' salaries were not keeping pace with their character's success, they knew a change needed to be made. Since they did not have much experience in show business, they searched for someone who did. By the time the girls turned four, their parents had fired their first agent and selected entertainment lawyer Robert Thorne to renegotiate the girls' contract.

Thorne was a veteran of the entertainment industry and had represented stars such as the rock musician Prince. He knew the girls were worth much more to the success of the show than the $4,000-per-episode wage they were currently receiving. Thorne met with producers and got them to give the girls more than six times that much, bringing their paychecks to a combined $25,000 per episode. He did not stop there, renegotiating several times as the girls' popularity grew. By the time *Full House* ended, Mary-Kate and Ashley were making a combined $80,000 per episode.

Beyond Television

A salary increase was not the only benefit of the girls' burgeoning popularity. When Parachute Publishing, a children's book publisher, saw how popular *Full House* was, it produced a paperback book based on the characters Michelle and Stephanie, one of her two older sisters on the show. Released in 1990, the book sold seventy thousand copies and became the first in the *Full House Sisters* series. The books were such a hit with young readers that separate series for the two sisters were introduced. The books about Michelle included the other *Full House* characters, but the stories were told from Michelle's perspective and pictured one of the Olsen twins on the cover. The books would continue to be popular even after the television series ended, with more than twenty-five titles focusing on Michelle.

The books showed that the twins had selling power outside of television, and soon more products were introduced that built upon interest in *Full House* and the five-year-old twins. A sixteen-

Full House Finale

Mary-Kate and Ashley were already busy with other projects during the final season of *Full House*, but they were still surprised and saddened when the series ended. The show did not end as many long-running series do, with a special episode that neatly completes the characters' story lines. Because there had been talk of doing a ninth season until actor John Stamos decided not to return, *Full House* simply ended with a regular show. As was the case in many of the episodes of the series's shows, the character of Michelle was the focus of what became the series finale. The hour-long show featured Michelle in a horseback riding competition. Because her father puts too much pressure on her to win, she rides her horse to a meadow where she is thrown from the horse, hurts her head, and loses her memory. Both twins appear in the show in a dream sequence, as Michelle tries to remember who she is. Her memory finally returns, and the show ends with a curtain call introduction for the cast members. The twins did not realize that this would be their last day of filming *Full House* until they were given flowers after shooting ended.

As their agent, Robert Thorne renegotiated the Olsen's television salaries on several occasions and helped the twins to capitalize on their popularity.

inch talking Michelle doll, with curly blonde hair pulled up in a bow at the top of her head, was sold in a pink box. One version of the doll was sold wearing a pink party dress, while another was dressed in jeans and a white shirt. The doll was followed by a board game and a series of smaller dolls featuring the entire *Full House* cast.

The girls had proven that they were popular with television viewers and could generate book and toy sales. However, their early popularity was always tied to their character on *Full House.* Thorne realized that it was not necessarily *Full House* or the character Michelle that the Olsens' fans loved, it was the girls themselves. For their next venture, the girls did not play the Michelle character; instead they began a project as Mary-Kate and Ashley.

Brother for Sale

In October 1992 the Olsen twins released *Brother for Sale,* their first music album for kids. In addition to the title track, in which the girls sing about their wish to sell their brother for fifty cents, they sang songs such as "Peanut Butter" and "Identical Twins." Although the girls did not have especially musical voices, the cute lyrics and their enthusiastic intonation were enough to capture the hearts of kids and their parents. *Brother for Sale* became one of the best-selling children's albums in the United States that year, selling more than three hundred thousand copies.

The five-year-olds followed *Brother for Sale* with another album, *I Am the Cute One.* Their second album featured the youngsters singing about which one was cuter and had them venturing into different musical genres such as hip-hop and rap. Critics, such as reviewer Ken Tucker of *Entertainment Weekly,* panned the album, saying, "This time around, a foolish attempt has been made to make the Olsens sound cool, with hip-hop beats and an occasional rapped lyric." Despite the poor reviews, kids loved it.

Following the success of their albums, Thorne decided it was only logical for the twins to let their fans see them singing the songs. In 1993 the pair released *Our First Video.* On the seven-song video, the twins introduced each song with a bit of clever banter, weaving comments about their family life into introductions for songs such as "Brother for Sale" and a tribute to their mom. They worked on dance steps for the video, but many shots show them just having fun, jumping around in an unchoreographed way. Aside from an appearance by Minnesota Twins baseball player Kirby Puckett (in a song about twins), the video contained no appearances by readily recognizable celebrities. The video relied on the girls' charm and energy to carry it off, and it worked. The video quickly rose to the top of Billboard's music video charts and stayed on the best-seller charts for 157 weeks.

To Grandmother's House We Go

It was clear that Mary-Kate and Ashley no longer needed *Full House* in order to be successful and that they both had enough charisma to warrant separate roles. A few episodes of *Full House* took advantage of the dual talent that the pair offered, and they both appeared in an episode that featured a look-alike cousin, as well as another in which Michelle dreamed she was talking to herself. However, these brief scenes really did not allow the girls to fully show what they were capable of doing together.

In 1992 the Olsen twins starred with Rhea Perlman and Jerry Van Dyke in their first television movie To Grandmother's House We Go.

It was their first television movie that gave them the chance to prove what they could do as a team. In the summer of 1992, when they were on hiatus from *Full House*, the twins made their first television movie, *To Grandmother's House We Go*. In addition to being three times as long as their weekly television show, the ninety-minute movie also gave each of the girls the opportunity to have a role all to herself.

Mary-Kate and Ashley played Julie and Sarah Thompson, twins whose nonstop squabbling gets on their tired mom's nerves. Feeling bad about being hard on their single mom, they try to give her a break by going to their grandmother's house by themselves. In the comedy they hitch a ride in a delivery truck and manage to foil a plan by not-so-evil crooks played by veteran comedy actors Rhea Perlman and Jerry Van Dyke. In addition, they win over a singing delivery man and help their mom find love.

The girls did not deliver stellar acting performances in the movie, but they easily captured a large audience when the program aired. *To Grandmother's House We Go* made the top 10 in the Neilsen ratings, beating the venerable television news show *Sixty Minutes* in the same time slot. The movie's success showed just how many viewers the girls could bring to a show.

Thorne did not let the movie's success pass by unnoticed. Mary-Kate and Ashley had each been paid $125,000 to appear in the movie, but Thorne felt they were worth more. The girls could pull in viewers, and more viewers meant that a show had higher ratings. This translated into dollars for the network, since it could charge advertisers more to promote their products during a show with a large viewing audience. Thorne used the fact the movie had generated high ratings to secure a lucrative deal for Mary-Kate and Ashley that involved more television movies. Under the terms of the deal, they would also have their own series after *Full House* ended.

Taking Control

Although Thorne had already secured a great deal of work for the twins, he continued to look for additional projects for them. The twins had been the stars of a television show and a movie, and

Mary-Kate and Horses

Since she was very young, one of Mary-Kate's favorite pastimes has been horseback riding. When she and her sister were preschoolers, they received ponies as Christmas presents. Mary-Kate began doing Western-style riding when she was five, and two years later she learned English-style, which involves wearing an English riding jacket and breeches.

When she was six, Mary-Kate fell in love with a miniature pony named Four-by-Four while the girls were in Vancouver, British Columbia, making the movie *To Grandmother's House We Go*. She talked to the pony and groomed him whenever she got the chance. Mary-Kate liked to talk about the horse even after the family returned to California, and one time tried to pack her bags and return to Vancouver to visit the pony.

Mary-Kate got to do some riding in *To Grandmother's House We Go*, and she also got to show her riding talent in an episode of *Full House*. She competed in English-style horseback riding well into her teens, winning blue ribbons and trophies.

their character was the basis for books and a doll, but they had not had creative control over these projects. They did not have input into the show's plotlines or the determination of who was cast alongside them in a film. The books and doll had a face that belonged to the Olsen twins, but even they carried the name of their television character. Thorne wanted the girls to have more creative control over projects in which they were involved.

He knew it was their popularity that had made the television show and movie such a hit and their faces that were making the other products so popular. He wanted them to be able to determine what type of television show they did after *Full House* and to help decide what types of characters they should play in movies. Thorne was looking beyond their *Full House* years to other, new projects for the appealing pair.

Dualstar

To allow the girls to have more input into the merchandise related to them, Thorne created the production company Dualstar Entertainment in 1993. Thorne was the CEO, and at age seven Mary-Kate and Ashley became the youngest executive producers in the history of the entertainment business. This move further

In 1993 Mary-Kate and Ashley both produced and starred in their second television movie Double, Double, Toil and Trouble.

increased the twins' power, as they now had a say in plotlines and casting for their movies. It also allowed for further expansion of their projects outside of television, such as more albums, videos, and books. Most important, it gave the girls control. Thorne wanted them to have the opportunity to one day move beyond acting, and he selected deals that would help him meet this objective.

Not everyone liked his idea of putting little girls in charge. Many people felt it was a risky move. If Mary-Kate and Ashley changed their minds and decided they no longer wanted to act, the whole business would be in jeopardy. Others resisted taking direction from a pair of girls in elementary school. Jeff Franklin had directed the twins in *To Grandmother's House We Go* and had been the creator of *Full House*. He wanted to be the executive producer of their second movie, but Thorne wanted the girls to be the executive producers instead. Franklin decided not to do the movie, *Double, Double, Toil and Trouble*, which was produced by Dualstar.

Others had no problem working with Thorne and the young executives. By the middle of 1993, Mary-Kate and Ashley had television, recording, and music video deals worth at least $10 million. As busy as they were, Thorne insisted they could be busier if they wanted to be. "We probably turn down nine out of ten requests for their services," he said. "We could be doing Saturday-morning cartoon deals, toy deals, merchandising deals, poster deals. But we're not interested in burning them out."[7]

Idolized by Young Girls

Mary-Kate and Ashley's media empire was rapidly expanding, but it was not based on their talent. They were not precocious actresses or exceptional singers. Rather, they had a likeable, wholesome image that drew people's attention. Friendship is a popular theme with young girls, and some thought the twins' success was due in part to the fact that they were each other's best friend. Others attributed it to a rise in multiple births; because more twins were being born, there was high interest in the Olsen twins. Whatever the reason for their success, one thing was certain: Thorne was not about to let the popular pair fade from the public eye.

The girls continued to capitalize on their popularity with young girls by appearing in television specials. *The Olsen Twins Mother's Day Special* and *How I Spent My Summer Vacation* were released in 1993, and *Christmas at Home with the Stars* was released the following year. They also made their third television movie, *How the West Was Fun,* and appeared in the movie *The Little Rascals* in 1994.

As their popularity grew, the Olsens began to star in an increasing number of television specials, such as The Olsen Twins' Mothers Day Special *of 1993.*

Extra Work

Making movies, albums, and videos meant the twins' schedule was getting more and more hectic. In addition to acting and recording, they also did promotional work. Fans were eager to see the pair and would line up for a chance to have their photo taken with the young girls. When Mary-Kate and Ashley went to a Las Vegas convention to promote their music video, they politely sat in a booth while retailers attending the convention stopped by to have their picture snapped with the twins. They also greeted fans in New York, Minneapolis, and San Diego, where people crowded into a Sea World stadium to get a glimpse of them in person.

The girls did not seem to mind the additional work of the promotional appearances. The girls were used to their unusual lifestyle and seemed unaffected by the attention they received. They were polite and remained oblivious to the stares they received when they walked across a room.

A Little Bit Normal

Amid all of the activity surrounding their videos, albums, and books, the twins tried to maintain friendships outside of show business and do things that other kids liked to do. To celebrate the success of one of their videos, they took eight friends out for hamburgers. The fact that they were different from the other kids in the neighborhood was still apparent, however, when they picked everyone up for the event in a limousine.

Their parents deserved much of the credit for keeping the girls' lives stable. Despite the fact that their children were amassing a great deal of money, David and Jarnette kept a tight rein on how much the girls were allowed to spend. Seven-year-old Mary-Kate pleaded for a stuffed tiger after seeing real ones onstage during a Siegfried and Roy show in Las Vegas, but her father firmly told her that she could not have one because it cost too much. They had to do chores in order to receive an allowance, which ranged from one dollar to five dollars, depending on how much they helped around the house. The money they earned from their television show, movies, and other products was put into trust funds, and they were not allowed to touch their earnings until they

Money Matters

By the time they were seven, millions of dollars' worth of business deals had been negotiated based on Mary-Kate and Ashley's work. However, the grade-schoolers did not comprehend the breadth of their fame. Because their parents put their earnings into a trust fund, they were not tempted to spend their large paychecks on candy or toys. The only money they received was an allowance that was based on the amount of work they did at home. They got one dollar if they did a poor job of completing their chores and five dollars if they finished everything.

One day their father thought they were beginning to catch on to the fact that they were making a substantial sum when Mary-Kate asked him if she had more money than he did. Just when he thought he would have to admit that she was making more money than her father ever would, he realized she was talking about the forty-five dollars she was keeping stashed away in her piggy bank.

The girls knew something about their financial situation, however. While making It Takes Two, their first big-screen movie, the director overheard them discussing money. Ashley thought it was likely that they were being paid five dollars a week. Mary-Kate thought it had to be much more than that—at least ten dollars.

turned eighteen. Business managers and outside attorneys oversaw the funds to make sure the money was not used improperly.

The End of *Full House*

The girls were too young to be motivated by money, but that did not keep them from being steadily employed. In fact, the twins were so involved with other projects that by the time the last episode of *Full House* was filmed in 1994, ending the show's eight-year-run, the eight-year-old Olsen twins were more than ready to move on to projects that featured them as individuals. While it was sad for the girls to say good-bye to the friends they had made on the show, they were not at a loss for things to do after the show ended. Some thought Mary-Kate and Ashley's careers would end with the show and that the millions of viewers who had watched them on *Full House* each week would soon forget about them. However, Thorne had prepared for the end of the series. He saw the end of the series as the girls' opportunity to do more with their music and videos, as well as books. The machinery was already in place to propel them to another level of stardom.

Chapter 3

Growing with Their Fans

Aᴩᴛᴇʀ *FULL HOUSE* ended, the twins wasted no time in getting back in front of the camera and their fans. They began acting in a series of mystery and party videos aimed at children, made their first feature film, and continued to record albums. Even though they were no longer part of a weekly television series, they were just as busy as ever. However, the girls, and their fans, were growing up. For Mary-Kate and Ashley, this opened up even more possibilities as they turned their changing interests into plots for their videos and another television series.

It Takes Two

Mary-Kate and Ashley's success to this point had come from television, holiday specials, and videos. They maintained a high popularity rating, and the next step was to see whether their charisma would carry over to the big screen. The girls made their big-screen debut the year after *Full House* ended. *It Takes Two* starred the pair as Alyssa Callaway and Amanda Lemmon. The identical strangers, one rich and one poor, meet at camp and decide to play matchmaker for Alyssa's rich father and Amanda's social worker mother. Big-screen stars Steve Guttenberg and Kirstie Alley had the major adult roles in the film, and while some screen time was devoted to their developing romance and its accompanying pitfalls, much of the attention was focused on the movie's charming twins.

Mary-Kate and Ashley's popularity was evident when the girls were recognized by fans while filming the movie in New York's Little Italy. Three school buses passed near the movie's set, and a few minutes later seventy-five screaming children stomped off the bus and ran over to get a glimpse of the girls. Moviemaking came to a halt as the fans swarmed the set. "They are an unexplainable phenomenon," said the film's director, Andy Tennant, who was amazed by the enthusiasm of the girls' fans.[8]

Despite the adoration of the girls' young fans, the movie earned just $19 million at the box office and did not establish the girls as big-screen stars. However, the girls' true marketing power came through videos, and when the movie was later released on video, it generated $75 million.

The Trenchcoat Twins

Dualstar decided not to worry about appealing to the general public and aimed Mary-Kate and Ashley's products straight at the hearts of young girls. The company's first venture in this area was a video series called *The Adventures of Mary-Kate and Ashley.* The girls played detectives nicknamed the Trenchcoat Twins in the series of thirty-minute mystery videos, which were introduced in 1994. The first in the series were *The Case of the Thorn Mansion* and *The Case of the Logical I Ranch.* Although the videos featured less-than-stellar acting, the mysteries successfully combined action, song, and the twins' charm. The first mystery videos proved to be so popular that four more were introduced in 1995, three in 1996, and one the following year.

The public could not seem to get enough of the twins. In 1995 Mary-Kate and Ashley became two of only a few entertainers who could release five movies and videos at the same time, a feat that would have been overkill for most performers. The girls had been busy putting out videos when the movie division of entertainment giant Warner Brothers decided to release two of their television movies, *To Grandmother's House We Go* and *Double, Double, Toil and Trouble,* on home video. Thorne convinced Warner's video and movie divisions to work together and release the movies at the same time as three new Olsen twin videos. This allowed the girls' videos to be promoted in the previews before the start of the movies. Warner agreed to Thorne's plan, and the movies were released at the same time as the videos *The Case of the Christmas Caper,*

The Adventures of Mary-Kate and Ashley

The girls' first video series featured Mary-Kate and Ashley as detectives called the Trenchcoat Twins, a nickname coined by agent Robert Thorne's wife. The girls played characters named Mary-Kate and Ashley Olsen in the video series and in a set of books based on the videos. The shows, which promised their fans mystery, action, and song, had them living by the motto that they would "Solve Any Crime by Dinnertime."

The videos had simple plotlines, such as the girls looking for a ghost in a haunted mansion or trying to find their dad's missing laptop computer. To keep their fans' attention, the videos included sight gags, cartoonish characters, and bits of dialogue interspersed with songs such as "Bravery" and "That Funky Musicology," sung by the twins. Almost like a live-action *Scooby-Doo*, the videos had "monsters" that turned out to be normal people and perpetrators that had to be unmasked. To parents' delight, the videos also introduced kids to a little deductive reasoning, as the twins tried to figure out the caper, and often included interviews with experts on topics ranging from volcanoes to space travel.

The series began in 1994, and their adventures included *The Case of the Sea World Adventure*, *The Case of the Fun-House Mystery*, *The Case of the Christmas Caper*, and *The Case of the U.S. Space Camp Mission*. The final video in the series, *The Case of the Volcano Mystery*, was released in 1997. Although the girls outgrew their private eye personas, the shows were rereleased in later years with multiple mysteries on one video.

The Olsen twins starred as young sleuths known as the Trenchcoat Twins in The Adventures of Mary-Kate and Ashley, *a series of video mystery capers.*

The Case of the Fun-House Mystery, and *You're Invited to Mary-Kate and Ashley's Sleepover Party.*

Hanging Out with Mary-Kate and Ashley

The video releases included the first in a new series called *You're Invited.* The series featured the girls singing, dancing, and having fun in settings such as a sleepover party, ballet party, Christmas party, and birthday party. The musical segments were loosely tied together with bits of banter between the girls.

The themes of the videos were based on things the girls liked to do and helped them continue to connect with their audience of young girls. It stood to reason that if they liked events such as birthday parties and sleepovers, then other girls their age did, too. By showing the girls enjoying things that other girls their age also liked, the videos consistently reinforced the girls' friendly image. In the videos they seemed more like a girl's next-door neighbors than untouchable stars.

The twins were not lauded for their acting ability, but their cute faces were irresistible to young girls who wanted to identify with them. They were also popular with parents who were looking for shows their children would enjoy. "They don't have exquisite talent," said Tennant. "What they have is a lot of charm and a huge marketing campaign. That's what sells these days."[9]

What the twins lacked in acting ability their company made up for with good business sense. While there were plenty of videos and other entertainment products aimed at families or boys, there was little competition for video dollars spent on young girls. Mary-Kate and Ashley's videos appealed to this market. By the time the girls were ten, their videos had sold more than 6 million copies, while their music video had sold an additional five hundred thousand. By 1997 their videos led the nonanimated children's market. The twins also continued to attract new fans through *Full House.* Although new episodes had not been made for years, the series had gone into syndication and repeats were shown regularly.

Mini-Millionaires

The popularity of the Olsen twins' media products was bringing in a nice sum of money to Dualstar. The girls earned royalties for the syndicated *Full House* episodes, and by 1997 Dualstar had collected $3 million for the work the girls had done on the series when they were younger. Their videos had brought in another $6 million.

Thorne was very careful to keep production costs for the videos low. Keeping costs to a minimum allowed each video to generate more profit. Cost-saving measures included using lesser-known actors and simple scenes. The videos did not include fancy special effects or appearances by other stars. In order to save money on transportation and lodging, the videos were set in locations that benefited other companies. The girls made videos at Sea World and Space Camp, on a cruise ship, and at a fancy hotel. The companies paid the cost of getting the girls to the location and allowed them to stay there free of charge. In return, the companies' names were mentioned frequently in the videos, giving them publicity that would be seen countless times by video viewers.

It took only about four or five days to shoot each video, which meant that several could be made during a single trip to a location. Mary-Kate and Ashley turned a trip to Hawaii into four videos: *You're Invited to Mary-Kate and Ashley's Hawaiian Beach Party, The Case of the Hotel Who-Done-It, The Case of Volcano Mystery,* and *The Case of the U.S. Navy Adventure.*

Deals such as these meant it cost only about $250,000 to make an Olsen twins video. By comparison, it took about $1.6 million to make a single episode of *Full House.* The cost of many movies runs into the millions of dollars. By spending as little as possible, Dualstar was able to make a huge profit on the videos it sold for $12.95 each.

Letting Thorne Take Control

As kids still in grade school, Mary-Kate and Ashley remained blissfully ignorant of the details of the business dealings surrounding their work and how much money they were bringing in. More than half the profits from Dualstar Entertainment were placed into a trust for the girls. While their parents were allowed to take out a small management fee, the rest of it would not become available to the girls until they reached age eighteen. The

In 1998 the Olsen girls pose for a publicity photo at the release of a series of books based on their Trenchcoat Twins characters.

girls had no idea how much money their products were bringing in. "People say to them: 'What's it like to be a millionaire?'" said their acting coach, Barbara Daoust. "They just get this glazed look on their face." [10]

Thorne controlled the business's day-to-day operations and kept tabs on Dualstar's cash flow. While they did not worry about the money Dualstar was bringing in, Mary-Kate and Ashley had some familiarity with the decisions that went into the business side of the entertainment industry. Profits and losses and balance sheets were beyond them, but by attending meetings with Thorne they realized that there was more to making a video than reciting their lines.

As nine-year-olds, the fourth graders had business meetings with Thorne at his fancy office in Century City, California. While they were not deeply involved with every aspect of the business, talking with him gave them an idea of what they would be doing

The twins credit their agent Robert Thorne with much of the success they enjoyed in the mid-1990s.

next. They had the opportunity to offer suggestions for video themes, so the videos they were making paralleled their real-life interests.

The girls quickly realized that the person who truly wielded power in any situation was Thorne. Even their father deferred to him on such simple subjects as the girls' hairstyles in promotional photos. Mary-Kate showed that she knew who to go to when she was asked to do an interview with a television crew. She had had a rough morning on the set and was getting frustrated with the interviewer's questions, so she asked for a phone. She called Thorne and told him that she did not want to do the interview anymore. Although there were plenty of other people around her that day, she realized that going to Thorne would get her out of an interview she was not enjoying.

The girls relied on Thorne to set the course for their careers, although they did not always grasp what his plans meant. The agent's goal for Mary-Kate and Ashley was to have them grow in their careers and become producers or directors one day. At this age they were not exactly sure what this would involve, and they were hesitant to give his plan their heartfelt approval. While meeting with a reporter at a restaurant in Los Angeles, they gave Thorne blank looks and fiddled with their french fries when he tried to get them to confirm his aspirations for them.

The pace he had in mind for the girls' careers was a hectic one. By age ten they had made more than 190 episodes of a television series, two top-selling children's albums, three TV movies, eight mystery videos, and the feature film *It Takes Two*. In the works were another television series, five more videos, and a fourteen-book publishing deal with Scholastic.

Trouble at Home

While Mary-Kate and Ashley were extremely busy making videos, their parents were going through some stressful times. David and Jarnette were divorced in early 1996 and got joint custody of Mary-Kate, Ashley, Trent, and Elizabeth. Soon after the divorce, David married a former coworker from his mortgage company. He and his wife, McKenzie, have two children, Taylor and Jake.

The breakup of their parents' marriage came at a time when the sisters were often making videos, and the hectic pace of their lives helped blunt the pain from the divorce. They had released

Dad's Remarriage

In one of the rare instances that the girls did not act in tandem, Ashley chose not to attend her father's wedding when he married their stepmother, McKenzie, soon after divorcing his wife. Ashley stayed home with her mother during the wedding, while Mary-Kate attended the ceremony. Their father's divorce, and the fact that Ashley did not attend the wedding, was splashed on the pages of tabloid newspapers.

Ashley did not remain bitter, however, and reconciled with her father. David and Jarnette shared custody of their four children, who split their time between the two households. When Mary-Kate and Ashley traveled to locations to make movies, their mother or father also went with them. "The reality is that the transition has been very smooth," their father said in an interview with Dana Kennedy in *Entertainment Weekly* a few months after the divorce. "Everyone sees eye to eye. The girls are fine."

a movie and five videos the year before their parents split up, and
they released three more the following year. "To be honest, we
were kind of busy at that point," Ashley said years later. "We had
so many people that loved us that we were like, 'That's okay.
Things will be better this way.' We were very mature for our age." [11]

Too Much?

While their full schedule helped keep the girls' minds off their
family's problems at home, some wondered if they were doing
too many projects at the same time. From a business perspective, they ran the risk of turning themselves into a fad, like the
Power Rangers or Pokemon, that children would lose interest in.
From a personal perspective, they risked burning out and having moviemaking become a grind. The girls insisted that they
loved making movies and would stop as soon as they were no
longer having fun doing it. "We've made a conscious effort to give
them a normal life," their dad said. "My kids are who they are.
They work in Hollywood but they don't live it." [12]

The girls found time for school, sleepovers, and ponies.
Because their movies were made through their own company, the
girls could decide when and where they were made. Unlike other
child stars, they did not have to go to auditions, compete with
other children for parts, and risk rejection every time an opportunity for a role came their way. As sisters, on the set they always had someone their age to relate to. They had the power to
accept or reject parts, and their opinions were welcomed. This allowed them to maintain a sense of control over their lives and careers. Because they had input into what they did and where they
went, they were always interested in doing more. "We ask them
about each project and only go ahead if they say yes," Thorne
said. "If they didn't want to act, they wouldn't." [13]

Thorne handled all publicity requests for the girls, and he was
aware that the girls risked being overexposed. In early 1997 he
told a *Wall Street Journal* reporter that they no longer did interviews for television talk shows because it would have been overkill,
even though stars such as talk show host Rosie O'Donnell badly
wanted the girls to appear. Even Thorne could be persuaded, however, and in April and October 1997 the girls were guests on

After Jarnette and David Olsen divorced in 1996, they shared joint custody of the twins. Here, David appears with his daughters at the premiere of the film Wild America.

O'Donnell's show. Thorne did turn down marketing opportunities such as the idea of putting the girls' faces on lunchboxes, and he nixed network specials that he said were poorly conceived. "That's exploitative," he said. "It doesn't build a career." [14]

Keeping It Real

Mary-Kate and Ashley's parents insisted that the twins were not being exploited. They noted that although they worked in Hollywood, they did not live a glamorous Hollywood lifestyle and were not pressured to act. "From very early on, it's been about controlling their environment," their father said. "It's not just throwing them to the wolves. They like acting. As soon as they stop enjoying it, it ends." [15] David and Jarnette worked hard to keep their daughters grounded, continuing to give the youngest self-made millionaires in history an allowance of five to ten dollars each week.

The girls were not prima donnas who thought only of themselves and expected others to cater to their whims. While on the set, they were accompanied by a nanny, tutor, and personal acting coach, and often a lawyer and marketing manager, but they did not become spoiled by all the attention. They worked about five months of the year, and at home they had friends who were not involved in show business. They went to a private school, had time to play with their friends, and enjoyed sleepovers. They went inline skating and visited amusement parks. Some kids at school and former costars were jealous of their success, but they did not seem to be bothered by what others thought. "We do everything other kids do," Mary-Kate said. [16]

Changing Interests

While the girls were doing as many normal childhood things as possible, at age ten the girls again reached a critical point in their young careers. They were outgrowing the simple plots of their *Adventure* videos and the *You're Invited* series. If their careers were to continue, they would have to make changes to the series to reflect their maturing interests and stay in touch with their audience.

The *You're Invited* series ran from 1995 to 2000 and followed a simple format, with dialogue interspersed with songs revolving around a theme. However, the themes changed as the girls grew older. When the Olsens were nine, the video series showcased a sleepover party, and at age eleven they invited fans to the Mall of America in Bloomington, Minnesota, and the New York Ballet. By age thirteen they were starting to think about boys and fashion, and they put out a *Fashion Party* video in 1999 and a *School Dance Party* video in 2000. In the *School Dance Party* video, they sing about whether or not to call a boy, sing in the bathroom about

In Style

At age ten Mary-Kate and Ashley began to gain a sense of fashion when they started working with designer Judy Schwartz. Schwartz was an executive designer who decided what clothing they would wear to public appearances and in videos. While at first Mary-Kate's idea of a nice outfit was anything paired with her tight, fringed shorts, and Ashley liked baggy clothes, Schwartz helped the girls get a feel for what clothing was in style and what looked good on them.

Schwartz also selected the clothing for the series *Two of a Kind.* The girls were twelve by that time and were more interested in looking like adults than kids. To fit their tastes, Schwartz took adult clothing and restyled it to fit them.

The girls got many questions from fans about where they could buy the clothing they wore on the television show or in videos. This gave Schwartz an idea. Since so many of their fans were interested in what they wore, she wondered about having the girls launch their own line of clothing. It would be a few years before their mary-kateandashley brand hit store shelves, but their sense of style was pointing the girls in yet another new direction.

boys, and sing about how puzzling boys are before it is suddenly time to clean up after the dance and they reflect on what a great time they had. While their videos continued to entertain with spunky music, they also made it clear that the girls were not little kids any more.

Two of a Kind

In addition to establishing the fact that they were growing up, the girls also wanted to promote their individuality. Although they again played twin sisters in their next project, the television series *Two of a Kind,* they began to focus on their differences. Although the show's title emphasized that they were a pair, their characters had separate interests. Mary-Kate played a tomboy who liked sports, while Ashley was interested in fashion, shopping, and boys. Set in Chicago, the show featured the girls as sisters with a college professor dad and a hip babysitter. The dialogue was more mature and emphasized the fact that the twelve-year-old twins were getting older, and the show tried to be cute but not sugary while looking at teen issues such as curfews and dating.

The series seemed to have everything going for it. It had the same producers as *Full House*, was on ABC just as *Full House* had been, and even had the same time slot as the earlier series. Although they had not been on a weekly television series for years, the girls were still very widely recognized by the public. "They have tremendous public awareness," said executive producer Michael Warren. "When I say I'm doing a show with the Olsen twins, it's always, 'Ooh, my kids love them.'" [17]

Despite their popularity, the show got middle-of-the-road reviews. *People Weekly* called it "contrived, synthetic and formulaic." [18]

In the television series Two of a Kind, *Mary-Kate and Ashley played twin sisters with very different personalities.*

The show's premise was criticized for being too much of a typical sitcom, with its starchy dad, free-spirited babysitter, and cute girls. The show was not horrible, but people did not get excited about it. It was cancelled after only eight months.

While the show was not a hit, it did set the stage for the next steps in the twins' career. They would begin to be seen more as individuals than a unit as they turned into teenagers. They were not just the Olsen twins; they were two young girls with separate personalities and interests.

Moving On

Mary-Kate and Ashley had hit some bumps in the last half of the 1990s, with the divorce of their parents, the remarriage of their father, and the cancellation of their new sitcom after only one season. However, they weathered the storm by staying busy and producing videos and movies that continued to please their young fans. They said they really did not think about their work and stardom; it had been part of their lives for so long that it was routine.

Some worried that they were doing too much, but they insisted that they loved the entertainment industry. Ashley said they would miss acting if they stopped, and they enjoyed returning to the set of a television show. "It's a lot of fun just to be back," she said while *Two of a Kind* was being made.[19] They and their company did not stop thinking of new ways to connect with girls their age. As they grew, Mary-Kate and Ashley continued to have their fingers firmly on the pulse of their fans and knew how to produce what they wanted, from albums to videos to fashion.

Chapter 4

Becoming a Brand

ALTHOUGH *TWO OF A KIND* had been cancelled after only one season, Mary-Kate and Ashley remained popular with young girls and their parents. As the twins entered their teen years, they looked for projects that would be enjoyed by kids their age but would not alienate their younger fan base. To bridge the gap between their youngest fans, who enjoyed watching the girls as preschoolers on *Full House*, and fans who were on the verge of becoming teenagers as the Olsens were, the twins made videos that reflected their maturing tastes and created the Mary-Kate and Ashley merchandise brand. The brand allowed the twins to market their image to girls of different age groups through clothing and jewelry as well as books and videos.

While the videos they had made at a younger age were still on the market and continued to be popular, the twins did not want to be thought of as six-year-olds forever. The pair did not belittle the work they had done as youngsters, and they continued to promote it, but they also recognized that they would need to put out products aimed at older kids if they were to have their fan base grow with them. As they grew up, Mary-Kate and Ashley were constantly reinventing their image while being careful not to stray from the basic values that had made them popular.

The twins moved gingerly away from the cute videos they had made when they were preschoolers and children, but they still espoused the wholesome, sporty, cheery image that had taken them to the top so many times before. Not hiding the fact that they were growing up, they began a series of feature-length videos and launched another television series. As young teens, their movies began to include the interests of girls their age, such as

46

boys and fashions, but still leaned toward lighthearted comic and adventurous fare.

Feature-Length Movies

Up until this time, the twins had been making short party and mystery videos. The half-hour videos had been geared toward the attention span of a younger audience and had featured the twins singing, dancing, and participating in an occasional chase scene. The videos' plots were usually constructed around a limited amount of dialogue. However, as their audience grew older, the twins wanted to do longer shows with more substantial story lines.

In 1998 Mary-Kate and Ashley began to make feature-length movies for television and video. Their first of these ninety-minute movies was *Billboard Dad.* Released in 1998, it featured Mary-Kate

In 1998 the success of the Olsen twins' first feature-length movie, Billboard Dad, *paved the way for additional movie projects targeting teen audiences.*

and Ashley as devoted daughters determined to find a wife for their widowed dad. To do so, they put up a wife-wanted poster on Sunset Strip—a popular and busy street in Hollywood. Their dad, an artist, endures a number of comic dates before falling in love. Of course, the courtship does not go smoothly, and Mary-Kate and Ashley must foil a plot by a dishonest art dealer before true love can prevail.

The movie's plotline was not especially deep or original, and it was not hard to figure out how it would end, but the movie proved that Mary-Kate and Ashley could handle longer scenes and sustain a ninety-minute film. The movie was their first feature-length film since they had made *It Takes Two* in 1995, when they were nine years old. Its success paved the way for a series of feature film–length television movies and videos starring the pair. The twins' interest in soccer inspired their next movie, *Switching Goals,* which was released in 1999. The movie originally aired on *The Wonderful World of Disney* and had the girls dealing with a sports-crazed dad and their different levels of athletic ability. They played twin sisters, Sam and Emma Stanton, who switch identities so they can be on certain soccer teams. The movie featured sports action on the soccer field and some comic moments as they tried to fool boys about their identities.

Traveling Girls

While *Billboard Dad* was made in California and *Switching Goals* was filmed in Canada, the girls' next movie took them halfway around the world to Paris, France. *Passport to Paris,* also released in 1999, was a milestone for the girls. It included a kissing scene, more difficult dialogue, and longer speeches than the girls had done in their previous movies, including a speech in French for Ashley. The girls made the best of these new challenges and worked hard at the language, trying to speak French as much as possible when they were in Paris. Ashley eventually pulled off her French-speaking scene, and *Passport to Paris* became the first in a successful series of adventure films made for the girls in exotic locations around the world.

One of the reasons for setting a movie in Paris was to keep the filmmaking process fun for Mary-Kate and Ashley. Their

First Kiss

In addition to being their first movie set at an exotic location, *Passport to Paris* also featured Mary-Kate and Ashley's first on-screen kisses. They were nervous and tense, but they did not have to fret about it too long, as the scene was filmed on the first day of the movie's production. Filming the kiss scene on the first day meant that they did not have to worry about it while doing other scenes, but it also meant the girls did not know their male costars very well. In fact, the thirteen-year-olds met them the day the scene was filmed.

If this was not enough to bring on anxiety, their mom was also there watching the shooting of the scene. Although she tried to boost their confidence by telling them how nice they looked and assuring them that it would all go fine, having her watching added another level of discomfort to the scene for the girls. Their knees were shaking and they had butterflies in their stomachs as they kissed boys they barely knew in front of a crew of fifty.

Although doing the scene was uncomfortable for them, they were experienced enough about making movies to know that not every scene would be a breeze. At thirteen, they had already developed a thick enough skin to know that they could not compromise the job they had to do because of worries about what others thought. "If you want to make movies you can't be afraid of being embarrassed," Mary-Kate told Damon Romine, the author of their biography, *Our Story*. "You have to do your job in front of a group of people. So you have to be ready to put yourself out there."

Starring in films such as Passport to Paris *allowed Mary-Kate and Ashley the opportunity to travel to exotic locales.*

movies had long paralleled their interests, from horseback riding to ballet to soccer, and now included a new one: travel. Allowing them to select exotic settings for their movies helped keep the girls' work interesting and enjoyable for them, and also proved alluring for their fans. Visiting Paris was only a dream for most young teens, and putting Mary-Kate and Ashley there was a marketing hook that worked. *Passport to Paris* went on to top the video sales charts the year it was released.

The girls chose Australia as the location for their next movie, *Our Lips Are Sealed*. In the comedy the girls are in the witness protection program to shield them from a criminal ring. They eventually foil the thieves, and along the way they learn to speak Australian slang, make new friends, and meet some boys. The comic adventure, released in 2000, is lighthearted and fun.

Keeping in Touch with Young Fans

Mary-Kate and Ashley's new videos were aimed at the young teens they had become. In addition to *Passport to Paris* and *Our*

The Olsen twins chose the sandy beaches of Australia as the setting for Our Lips Are Sealed, *their second feature-length movie.*

Lips Are Sealed, two more videos were released in the *You're Invited* series in 1999 and 2000. While the new videos reflected the girls' changing interests, they did not forget about their younger fans. They continued to put their maturing faces on collections of videos they had made when they were younger.

In 2000 a ninety-minute collection of their party videos, called *You're Invited to Mary-Kate and Ashley's Greatest Parties,* was released. Although it featured the fourteen-year-old twins on the cover, the three videos on the tape had been made a few years earlier. Repackaging their camping party, costume party, and fashion party videos on the same tape allowed the girls to reach new fans with the same material and package it in a longer format that was more appealing to older kids. They used a similar technique to package three of their Trenchcoat Twins stories on the video *The Amazing Adventures of Mary-Kate and Ashley,* and in 2001 they released another package with a holiday theme, *Mary-Kate and Ashley's Christmas Collection.*

Mary-Kate and Ashley in Action!

No matter how many different ways the girls repackaged their videos, no one could control the fact that the girls were growing and changing. They would eventually be too old to put their faces on the cover of videos they made when they were younger. There was, however, one entertainment medium where they would never have to grow old: cartoons. In October 2001 they entered the world of animation with *Mary-Kate and Ashley in Action!*

The cartoon used the pair's voices and cast them as crime fighters. Ashley voiced Special Agent Amber, while Mary-Kate was the voice behind Special Agent Misty. They fought off such evildoers as pet hater Fritz Doberman, who makes people neglect their puppies by inventing the perfect robotic dog, and Clive Hedgemorton Smyth, who attempts to steal all of the world's horses for himself. The cartoon gave the girls the opportunity to step back and please their younger fans while being vague about their age.

Fashion Dolls

Not restricting themselves to videos, cartoons and movies, Mary-Kate and Ashley also continued to lend their images to a pair of fashion dolls. Made along the same lines as a Barbie doll, the dolls had the girls' features and fashions. Initially sold with shorter hairstyles, the dolls were retooled in 2002 to give them the longer hair that Mary-Kate and Ashley were wearing at the time. Although they were priced higher than many similar fashion dolls, they were a hit and quickly rose to become Mattel's number 2 selling fashion doll, outsold only by Barbie herself.

mary-kateandashley

A stylish fashion doll was not the only way Mary-Kate and Ashley were expanding their marketing reach beyond television and videos. Ever since their television series *Two of a Kind* had generated interest in what they were wearing, there had been plans to introduce a fashion line with the girls' names on it. These plans came to fruition in January 2001, when the fourteen-year-old twins introduced the mary-kateandashley brand.

The stylish Mary-Kate and Ashley dolls were very popular with fans of the Olsen twins.

The initial fashions in the line included peasant blouses and other '70s-inspired designs aimed at girls ages six to eleven. The twins and their fashion stylists proved to be on the mark with consumers, and their low-rise pants in stylish colors were an especially big hit.

The mary-kateandashley brand was initially sold only at retail discount giant Wal-Mart. Because Wal-Mart is known more for low prices than high-quality merchandise, selling their blouses and pants only through the discounter could have given the impression that their clothing line was cheap and poorly made. However, pricing it a few dollars above the typical Wal-Mart merchandise gave the impression that the clothing was a step above the rest. Selling through a large, national discount retailer gave the mary-kateandashley brand instant access to the pocketbooks of millions of young girls and their parents. Like their movies, videos, and albums, their clothing was not designed to be extremely sophisticated or expensive. It was aimed at ordinary girls who wanted to identify with the wholesome, adventurous image Mary-Kate and Ashley projected. The fashion line was so popular that it accounted for a third of the $550 million Mary-Kate's and Ashley's names generated in 2001.

Connected with Their Brand

In addition to clothing, the mary-kateandashley name was placed on a number of other products. Their brand featured makeup, jewelry, pillows, and other accessories. By launching the fashion line and other items under the mary-kateandashley brand, the

In 2004 three young girls model the mary-kateandashley line of clothing featured in Wal-Mart stores across the country.

girls became more than just successful teens. Their wholesome image itself became a brand something outside themselves, yet very connected with them. "They are a property now, aside from being people with a heartbeat,"[20] said Thorne, who remained CEO of Dualstar Entertainment and continued to handle the direction of the twins' careers.

At an expo in Los Angeles in 2000, Mary-Kate and Ashley sign autographs and promote video games based on their books and television shows.

Thorne saw where Mary Kate and Ashley's products would fit in the marketplace, and he worked to generate exposure for the brand. However, he still gave Mary-Kate and Ashley credit for being the force behind the company. While the teens readily admitted that they were not exactly sure how the fashion merchandising deal with Wal-Mart had come about, Thorne insisted that they were the company's leaders. "Even though they're 14 years old, I work for them," he said. "It started as fiction, to be candid, that it was Mary-Kate and Ashley's deal, this brand, this whole thing. They were involved more like, 'Is this O.K.?' 'Sure.' Now they say we created a monster, but I don't think so, I think we created two professional executives."[21]

The twins had veto power over things they did not want to promote, and they turned down products they deemed too young. They dismissed Olsen Twins fruit snacks and wrapping paper, and they also nixed birthday party appearances. Because they wanted to make sure the products met their standards, they helped select the fabrics and designs for their fashion line. However, while the girls were encouraged to give their opinions, it was Thorne who was the driving force behind their business ventures. "Our business plan is that I decide which direction we are going to go, and we do it,"[22] he said.

Creating the mary-kateandashley brand seemed to be a logical move for the pair, whose fans admired their fashion sense. However, by agreeing to put their names and faces on items ranging from clothing to bracelets, Mary-Kate and Ashley took on more responsibility. Allowing products to carry their names also meant that sales would depend a great deal on how the public continued to perceive them. They would have to maintain their shiny image as well as their popularity.

A Few Misses

The girls' fashion line was a hit, but they also introduced a few projects in 2001 that did not work out. The girls became editors in chief of the *Mary-Kate and Ashley* magazine, which focused on building self-esteem. The magazine was aimed at teens and included articles on fashion, music, movies, sports, yoga, and boys and had a darker and more somber tone to it than their cheery, upbeat videos. Priced at six dollars an issue, it initially sold well; however, sales eventually dropped off. The venture was put on hold after three issues when the publishing company behind it went out of business.

This was not the only Olsen product to be taken off the market that year. *Mary-Kate and Ashley in Action!* was canceled in November 2002 after twenty-six episodes and a year on the air.

From London to the Bahamas

Not ones to dwell on things that did not work out, the pair did not skip a beat and continued to put out feature-length films that went directly to video. They introduced a pair of videos in 2001, *Winning London* and *Holiday in the Sun,* which took the sisters to England and the Bahamas. Incorporating boys, adventure, and fashion into the storylines, the videos broke little new ground for the girls in terms of their acting styles. However, the videos allowed them to continue to put out fare that was interesting and watchable for young girls. "With Mary-Kate and Ashley you can't go wrong," said director Craig Shapiro. "You put them in a fun situation and they are fun to watch."[23]

Winning London revolved around a model United Nations competition. These competitions bring students from around the world together to discuss international issues. In the video Mary-Kate and Ashley were part of a team of students that went to London to see which team knew the most about the country they represented and could best use problem-solving skills. The movie combined serious and lighthearted moments, as the girls discussed issues such as nuclear weapons and terrorism and tried to make a guard laugh at Buckingham Palace. They mixed in some romance and action scenes as well, including a chase sequence through a heating duct.

While *Winning London* had more of an educational feel, *Holiday in the Sun* was like a summer vacation. Filmed during a summertime trip to the Bahamas, the movie featured Mary-Kate and Ashley as a pair of sisters who foil a smuggling ring. Because the

Winning London in Style

Winning London allowed the girls to explore slightly different themes than they had in the past, and it had a bit more of an educational bent than the girls' previous feature-length videos. In the movie Mary-Kate and Ashley play a pair of sisters from California who are chosen to participate in a model United Nations conference. The movie's conference brought together teens from all over the world to discuss issues facing the various countries. Mary-Kate is Chloe Lawrence, a free-spirited girl who comes to London mostly to try to catch the eye of a boy who had long been just a friend. Ashley plays Riley Lawrence, who is intensely interested in winning the competition. With the theme that it is cool to be smart, the movie's setting allowed them to weave tidbits about England's history into the script and showcase London landmarks as backdrops for its scenes. "We were looking for some material that would be older for the girls and would not be like a light comedy," director Craig Shapiro said in the commentary included on the *Winning London* DVD.

In *Winning London,* the girls also moved away from the buddy films they had done in the past. In *Billboard Dad, Passport to Paris,* and *Our Lips Are Sealed,* the sisters they portrayed were best friends. In *Winning London,* they were more competitive, with different personalities, goals, and agendas.

In addition to taking on opposite personalities in the movie, the girls also sported distinct looks. Mary-Kate wore her hair straight, with a '70s feel and lightly feathered look. Ashley's longer hair was curly. They both agreed on the movie's fashions, however. With the help of a fashion stylist, they selected the clothing they would wear for their twenty-five costume changes in the film and came up with a fall European look that included hats, sweaters, and boots.

movie was filmed during the summer, they did not have to worry about schoolwork and found time to hang out by the pool, play on the beach, and get to know the other cast members. "We all just clicked," Mary-Kate said. "By the end of filming the group was really tight." [24]

The movie was made at a resort during the height of the tourist season, and while that was fun for the girls, it also presented a few problems. The girls spent so much time talking to fans and signing autographs that they were sometimes late to the set. One morning the producer tried to fool fans by having Mary-Kate wear a big hat and sunglasses, but a group of girls in the hotel lobby said hello to her as soon as she walked in. Mary-Kate and Ashley's faces had been recognizable since they were preschoolers, and their steady work did not allow them the luxury of anonymity.

So Little Time

Their work also meant that their time had to be carefully managed if they were to fit in filming, school, their fashion business, and a little time for themselves. The girls' movies were made at a fast pace, which allowed them to complete many projects in a year. They spent three and a half weeks filming on location in Paris and then finished the indoor shots for *Passport to Paris* in California. They used their summer vacation both to relax and to make *Holiday in the Sun* at the resort where they were staying. When they launched their next series, *So Little Time,* in 2001, they shot more than one episode in four days while at the same time spending three hours a day with an on-set tutor.

The idea for *So Little Time* was generated while the girls were on location in London. They heard the British pop group Arkana's peppy, upbeat song "So Little Time" and liked it so much that they chose it as the theme for their new series, which focused on the girls as a pair of busy high school students. The title also aptly

The Music of *So Little Time*

In contrast to the videos the twins had produced when they were younger, neither the series *So Little Time* nor their feature-length movies featured the twins singing. Instead, they featured upbeat songs by other artists. The song selections that were heard on *So Little Time* were also made available on CD. This was very much in keeping with Dualstar's philosophy of not missing a beat when it came to marketing, and the CD received positive reviews from fans of the show.

The title song for the show *So Little Time* was chosen by the twins after the tune by the British group Arkana caught their attention while they were making *Winning London.* The peppy song is along the lines of the *Friends* theme, "I'll Be There for You." It aptly captures the spirit of Mary-Kate and Ashley's characters in the show, who want to live their high school years to the fullest. Many of the other songs on the show's soundtrack have a rock feel to them, including "Mr. Fabulous" by the Australian band Noogie.

reflected the girls' hectic schedules and the precious few years they had left before they entered adulthood.

In *So Little Time,* the girls kept the characters' names from their *Winning London* video. However, this time fourteen-year-old Mary-Kate played the more academically oriented Riley, while Ashley was the free-spirited Chloe. The show focused on the sisters juggling school, boys, and the latest fashions. They did things they thought kids would love to do—such as form their own rock band—and could laugh at, such as a volunteer project that did not go as planned. They also dealt with an unconventional family. Their parents were separated, and their dad lived a laid-back life in a trailer while their businesslike mother lived in a classy beach house. A male housekeeper helped the family hold everything together.

The comedy was launched on Fox's Family Channel in 2001. The channel had already been showing reruns of *Two of a Kind* and *Mary-Kate and Ashley's Adventures* more than twenty times a week, and consistently pulled in good ratings. The channel wanted to use the series to help it establish a niche in the industry, as a channel kids would watch when they were too old for Nickelodeon but too young for MTV.

As executive producers of the show, Mary-Kate and Ashley were the first teens to produce and star in their own television series. They helped come up with the show's premise and were involved with its casting, scripts, and wardrobe. They did not always use their power to portray themselves in the best light. One of the show's running gags was that the sisters had a hard time getting boys to notice them, except for a geeky friend played by Jesse Head, who had a perennial crush on Mary-Kate's character. In real life, the girls did go on dates and were invited by boys to prom and other school dances. Ashley began dating Matt Kaplan during her freshman year, and he became her steady boyfriend throughout high school.

The show was not intended to mirror their real life but was a chance for the girls to try a different kind of comedy. The show included typical sitcom moments of banter between the girls and their on-screen parents, but also featured scenes in which the girls spoke directly to the camera and did physical comedy, such as sliding across the floor in a puddle of chocolate sauce and ice cream. The television series met with some critical acclaim when, in 2002, fifteen-year-old Mary-Kate was nominated for a best actress Emmy. In addition to being a compliment for her acting ability, the nomination also meant that the industry was beginning to recognize Mary-Kate and Ashley as individuals. However, after making twenty-six episodes the pair decided not to continue with the show because of their commitment to making another feature film before they finished high school. The show did not disappear after the last episode aired, however. As they had done so successfully with their others movies, their television series was put out on video and DVD.

Staying Cool

Putting the series out on video was an obvious move for a pair of stars who continued to remain popular with their target audience of girls between the ages of four and fourteen, who had spending power and were buying their brand. Their movies continued to cluster at the top of Billboard's video charts, and 30 million copies of their books were in print. While Mary-Kate's Emmy nomination was the first recognition either of the girls had received for their talents, their video and business ventures were decidedly a financial hit. Their businesses generated $500 million in retail sales in 2001, and the figures were expected to keep rising.

The girls did not want to be viewed as spoiled rich kids, however, and were careful to put forward a frugal image. When an article in The *New York Times Magazine* described their trip to a swank clothing store in Los Angeles, it emphasized the fact that Ashley was allowed to buy only one tank top and was told that she should consider buying a pair of jeans at an outlet store rather than the department store because they were less expensive there. They also did not want to appear to be conceited. Mary-Kate asked that the blue ribbons she won in horse shows not be emphasized in a *Los Angeles Times* article, because she did not want others to think she was bragging.

Mary-Kate and Ashley worked hard to project an image that resonated with girls their age, but at the same time they could not

In 2002 Mary-Kate (left) was nominated for a best-actress Emmy for her role in So Little Time. *She poses here with her sister at the Emmys.*

please everyone. They were still popular with younger girls, but teens had some reservations about giving Mary-Kate and Ashley's products their wholehearted approval. Despite the television show and videos aimed at a slightly older audience, the pair still did not rank as well with teens, who were a little more picky about what they considered cool. Mary-Kate and Ashley had some work ahead of them if they wanted to expand their audience base, but change was nothing new to them. They had been reinventing their image since they were preschoolers.

Chapter 5

Juggling It All

M ARY-KATE AND ASHLEY'S careers continued to move along smoothly as they entered high school, but as maturing teens they also had to deal with new pressures. They wanted to do well on their SATs, get into the colleges they desired, and have the freedom to spend time with their friends. They had never lived a celebrity lifestyle, but they were too well known to keep their personal lives private. They were aware that if they did not do well in school or were rejected by a university it could become a publicized piece of celebrity gossip. In addition, any activities they participated in with their friends could become public news. This added more stress to their lives as they became more aware of the responsibility they had to uphold their image.

Turning Sweet 16

The next milestone in Mary-Kate and Ashley's lives was their sixteenth birthday, and they looked forward to exerting a new sense of independence as they got older. They could not wait to get their driver's licenses and have the freedom that came with being able to go where they pleased and not have to rely on others for transportation. For girls who had been taking direction for almost all of their lives, a little bit of freedom was a welcome change.

The pair took their tests for their driver's licenses on their sixteenth birthday. Both passed, although Mary-Kate was tired from being awake for most of the night because of anxiety over the test. Their family also recognized that this was a milestone event in the girls' lives and their celebration had begun early in the morning with breakfast brought into their bedrooms, as video cameras captured the moment. After taking their tests, the girls thought they

High School Classmates

In addition to working on movies and selecting fashion designs, Mary-Kate and Ashley also went to high school. They attended Campbell Hall, a private school in North Hollywood. Among their classmates were other children who were connected to the entertainment industry.

Having classmates whose parents were actors, directors, and famous producers meant that the Olsens were in the same economic and social circles as their classmates. Attending school with their peers helped the girls adjust to high school, stay grounded, and enjoy the time they could spend with their friends. With their friends at school, they did not have to worry about living up to their image. "At the school we go to in Los Angeles, I can be myself and not worry about the business part of life," Ashley told Carrie Bell in an interview for *Teen People.* The only thing the twins were sometimes teased about was their petite stature (Ashley is 5-foot-2, Mary-Kate is 5-foot-1).

Mary-Kate and Ashley said they were not treated any differently from other students at school. The twins missed a significant number of classes while they were making movies but kept up with their schoolwork with the help of an on-set tutor. While making a television show or movie, they spent at least three hours each day in a makeshift classroom working with the tutor. They said there was competition between them to see who could get better grades and noted that if one twin did better on a test, the other would go over the subject again to bring her grade up.

Mary-Kate (left) and Ashley graduated from their private high school on June 11, 2004.

were going out with their boyfriends at the time for a quiet dinner at a restaurant. Instead, they were surprised by eighty of their closest friends and family members with a big party, complete with cakes shaped like California driver's licenses with their pictures on them. As a gift they each received a brand new Range Rover to drive.

Following their birthday Mary-Kate and Ashley released another feature-length video. While previous videos had shown their changing interests as they aged, they had not specifically mentioned how old they were. That changed with *Getting There*. Released in 2002, it had the subtitle *Sweet 16 and Licensed to Drive*.

In the movie the girls play Kylie and Taylor Hunter, a pair of sisters trying to get to the Olympic Winter Games in Salt Lake City, Utah. Along the way the pair gets split up, and the movie follows their separate adventures. With this story line, the two had the chance to act in separate scenes for a good portion of the movie. They each had an opportunity for plenty of outdoor action as well, including skiing, snowmobiling, snowboarding, and other winter activities designed to give the movie a hip, youthful feel. An eclectic array of camera angles and an upbeat soundtrack also give the movie an edge, but the predictable story line is much like the girls' previous films.

When in Rome

The other movie the pair released in 2002 had a more refined feel to it and returned the sisters to a foreign location. In *When in Rome* Mary-Kate and Ashley play students from California who spend a summer working as interns at a design firm in Italy. The twins uncover a plot planned by an ill-tempered and bitter adult. In the movie, the girls are set up to fail and lose their fashion internships. Luckily, the rich owner of the design firm comes to their rescue, and along the way they catch a thief who is stealing his designs and selling knockoffs. In addition, they meet a couple of boys and teach them the value of hard work.

Though *When In Rome* followed the well-known pattern of their earlier work, it reflected the interest the pair had in their own fashion line. In addition, as with their other movies set in foreign locations, the movie gives viewers glimpses of the highlights of the city, such as the Trevi Fountain, the Colosseum, and Spanish Steps. While the movie had a little more substance than *Getting There,* it was more lighthearted than serious.

Part of the Gang, Sort Of

Both *Getting There* and *When in Rome* showed Mary-Kate and Ashley as part of a large group of friends, an image they felt their fans would embrace. They wanted to be seen as normal teenagers who liked to hang around with their friends and have adventures, as in *Getting There,* or who tried new things and made new friends along the way, as in *When in Rome.* The pair did not want to appear to be snobbish or unapproachable, and they willingly signed autographs when fans recognized them.

In their movies and in interviews, Mary-Kate and Ashley were careful to emphasize how normal their lives were. In *Getting There,* it was their characters who had a car, but it was another character whose father had both an airplane and a yacht at his disposal.

The twins have always tried to make themselves accessible to their fans. Here, they sign autographs at a screening of their film New York Minute.

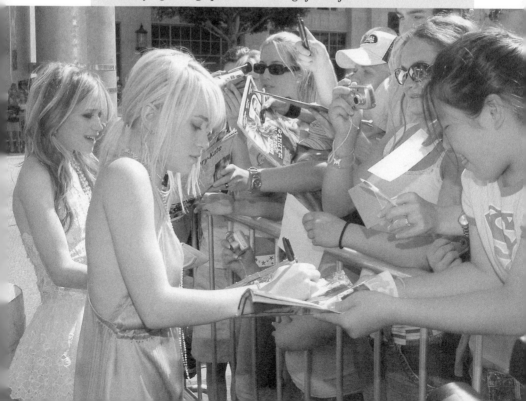

In their biography, *Our Story,* which was released in 2000 and updated in 2003, they continued to emphasize to their fans that they liked to do normal things such as hanging out at friends' houses or going to the beach. Ashley pointed out that they went to school and spent time with their friends and boyfriends. They went shopping and saw movies, stayed in shape with exercise and were especially fond of yoga.

The girls spoke highly of their family but stressed that they were not perfect. They noted that arguments sometimes broke out over the remote control, and they sometimes disagreed over who got to wear which outfit to an event.

They were also careful to show that they did not take their lifestyle for granted. When Mary-Kate recalled one of their first limo rides in their autobiography and noted what a big deal it had been at the time, Ashley quickly added, "I still feel kind of special when I get to ride in a limo."[25] While they did get special perks, such as invitations to Vanity Fair's Oscar party in 2002, like most teens, they were too shy to talk to stars such as Cameron Diaz and Gwyneth Paltrow.

A New Understanding

While they liked to think of themselves as ordinary teens, Mary-Kate and Ashley were also coming to a new level of understanding about how different their lives really were. To this point, they had simply accepted what happened in their lives and did not think of it as anything special. After all, they had been acting since the age of nine months, had grown up in front of the camera, and had become used to working in exotic locations such as London and the Bahamas.

However, as they matured, they began to have a different view of their world. As Mary-Kate watched a fashion show come together in Toronto in spring 2003, she realized how different and special her life was. "I was watching the whole set come together, and I couldn't believe it was real," she said. "It was the first time I really stepped back, and I was like, I'm so lucky to be here. I just looked at Ashley and said, 'This is so cool.'"[26]

Recognizable Costars

During their teen years, Mary-Kate and Ashley's movies often featured them interacting with a large group of friends. They drove to Utah with a group of teens in *Getting There*, sorted through a fashion industry mystery with a group of interns in *When in Rome*, and competed with other young adults in *The Challenge*. Although most of the other actors and actresses in their movies were not big stars, there were a few recognizable faces.

Among these teens were Amy Davidson and Billy Aaron Brown. Davidson had a recurring role as a ditzy waitress in *So Little Time* and went on to be part of a sitcom family in the network show *8 Simple Rules*. Brown was included in the group of friends in *Getting There*, was in *Holiday in the Sun*, and made a cameo appearance in *The Challenge*. He went on to play Davidson's love interest, Kyle, on *8 Simple Rules* and also appeared in an episode of *So Little Time*.

Mary-Kate and Ashley's Italian costar in *When in Rome*, Michelangelo Tomasso, was already a star in Italy when he took the role in their movie. The soap opera star actor was more well known in his native country than the Olsens were, and one day while they were shooting a scene in Rome a group of girls asked if they could have their picture taken with Michelangelo, requesting that Mary-Kate get out of the shot. Mary-Kate understood why he was so popular. In the movie her character has a crush on Tomasso's character Paolo, and in a scene where they bumped into each other and she fell into his arms, Mary-Kate forgot her lines when she looked into his eyes.

She and her sister had access to places other teens could only dream about, but at the same time the girls had parents who chose not to spoil them. Their business was run by a group of people who took the girls' feelings and ideas into account. In addition, they had enough influence over their careers to make their everyday lives fun and interesting, with trips to far-flung locations and fashion consultations. They could change the course of their fashion line or company simply by offering their opinion, and they were not challenged to provide facts or market research statistics to back up their approval or rejection of a particular product. Their lives had been busy to this point, but they had managed to get through things without a great deal of stress. As they grew older, however, they would face situations over which they had little control, such as college admissions and their continued march toward independence.

The Challenge

In fall 2003 the twins ended an era when *The Challenge,* the last in their series of straight-to-video movies, was released. Much like their other recent movies, it featured them in an exotic location having an adventure with other teens. This time they were in a *Survivor*-style game, and had to endure such tests as eating worms, standing on a post surrounded by water, and climbing over a swinging rope bridge.

As in *Winning London* and *When in Rome,* they played characters with different goals. Ashley's Lizzie was intense and academic, while Mary-Kate's Shane was more interested in saving the environment. This time their characters did not just have different personalities, however; they could not stand each other. They played the children of divorced parents who lived on opposite coasts and had not spoken for years. While the more intense conflict between them was a change from past movies, the film still followed a predictable pattern and used the well-worn theme of putting aside differences to work together toward a common goal.

After the completion of their final video, the pair were ready to take the next step in their careers. They were set to return to the big screen for the first time since their movie *It Takes Two.* "We've enjoyed a decade in video and DVD movies for younger audiences," Mary-Kate said. "Now we're ready to make the big screen our home as producers and actresses." [27]

The twins appeared to be solidly in control of their careers. Things were falling nicely into place when they got a call from Drew Barrymore asking them to appear in 2003's *Charlie's Angels: Full Throttle.* Although their cameo role was a brief appearance as themselves, it marked one of the few times they appeared in a movie not produced by their own company. The fact that they were offered the small role showed that other people in the movie industry appreciated their celebrity status, even though they had done little work outside of their own movies and videos. The recognition gave them confidence as they looked to make a leap from videos to the big screen. They planned to release their first big-screen movie in a decade around the time they graduated from high school.

School and Work

The pair could not concentrate solely on their careers, however. They had their hearts set on attending an East Coast school and were determined to get the grades and SAT scores that would get them admitted. The pressure they placed on themselves to do so, along with their work schedule, added stress to their lives in their last years of high school. They put their studies first and even turned down an appearance on *Oprah* to study for their SATs.

It was not easy for them to put aside their working lives. Their childhood had been such a mixture of work and play that it was sometimes difficult for them to put it all into perspective. They had been so conscious of putting out a positive public image for so long that they were not certain how to approach college admissions essays that asked questions about their personal lives. Application questions sent them turning to college counselors for advice. "We don't want to bring our work life into our school life, but then what do we say for a question like, 'Have you ever had a paying job before?'" asked Mary-Kate, noting that they had done videos, movies, dolls, and fashion lines. "Honestly, what are we supposed to say?"[28] She and her sister certainly had earned a great deal of money in their young lives but were at a loss to concisely explain exactly how they had done so.

Taking Care of Business

While they tried to downplay the work and business sides of their lives, Mary-Kate and Ashley were still intimately involved with their growing company. They did not initiate the business discussions that led to the development of their products, but they had become experts at offering their opinion and remained firmly committed to influencing products that carried their name. "If we feel strongly enough to say no to something then that's what happens," Mary-Kate said. "It's our line, it's our names and our brand—it's coming from us, Mary-Kate and Ashley. I've learned that 'No' is a full sentence."[29]

While Thorne still made the day-to-day decisions for Dualstar, Mary-Kate and Ashley were exercising more creative control over their movies. At one casting session, one of the partners tried to

In June 2002 Mary-Kate and Ashley demonstrate their business savvy as they speak about their clothing line at a Wal-Mart shareholders meeting.

get Mary-Kate and Ashley to agree to hire a lower-cost actor. However, Mary-Kate and Ashley exercised their creative control and decided who to hire. "I was like, Whoa. They grew up in that meeting," Thorne said.[30]

Their ability to veto products was not slowing down the volume of deals Dualstar was making. In spring 2003, nine albums they had recorded between 1992 and 2002 were reissued. The mary-kateandashley brand now included fragrances, mary-kateandashley one and mary-kateandashley two, scents they had personally chosen. The twins chronicled their senior year in high school with a series of articles in *Teen People* in which they talked about their excitement over senior-year dances and anxiety over their SATs, as well as promotional bits for their new movie.

Getting Accepted to College

While the girls were looking forward to their final year of high school, they missed much of the fall semester shooting *New York Minute,* their first theatrical release since *It Takes Two.* They were concerned with their grades and wanted to enjoy their final year of high school, but they also had to honor a commitment to make a theatrical movie before they entered college. While they loved working on location in New York City, they also lived with the tension of wondering whether or not they had been accepted into the college of their choice. They had their eye on a New York school but did not want to jinx their chances by leaking the name of the school to the media. They felt additional pressure was on them because if they did poorly on their tests or did not get into the school they wanted, the information could be leaked to newspapers and they would be embarrassed by it.

They got their answer in December 2003, when they learned that they had been accepted into New York University. "I was nervous because it was the only place I wanted to go, and I didn't have any backup schools," Mary-Kate admitted. [31] While they had been looking forward to college as a time to explore and try new things, they would not stray too far from the familiar, as they planned to attend the same college within New York University and live together. Their working lives would also follow them. A Dualstar office would be set up in New York so they could continue to be involved with the business while they were in college, and Thorne still had plans for them to star in movies, produce feature films, and take their brand worldwide.

Changing Identities

While their private lives would remain intertwined, Mary-Kate and Ashley took an initial step toward establishing separate public personas. Although they still planned to work together, a press release asked reporters to no longer refer to them in print as the Olsen twins. They wanted to be mentioned by their separate names as part of an attempt to avoid being thought of as a single unit forever. In addition, they began sporting different hair colors, with Ashley going blonde and Mary-Kate dying her hair reddish-brown.

Their request to be known as Mary-Kate Olsen and Ashley Olsen instead of the Olsen twins was also an attempt on their part to exhibit a more mature image. They still kept their wholesome, clean-cut look, however, and tried to represent a clean lifestyle. They stayed away from the Hollywood club scene, preferring to spend time with their friends to the wilder side of the entertainment industry. However, as Mary-Kate and Ashley neared age eighteen they began to deal with some unwanted attention from men who wanted them to grow up a little too fast. There were several Web sites set up that counted down the days until they became of legal age at eighteen. While they wanted to exhibit a more

As Mary-Kate and Ashley approached the age of eighteen, the twins tried to project a more grown-up image.

Featured in People *magazine after they turned eighteen, the grown-up Mary-Kate and Ashley continued to captivate fans of all ages.*

grown-up image, they tried to find a balance between growing up and maintaining their clean-scrubbed image. Their new movie would show them clad only in towels, but they turned down an offer to pose for the men's magazine *Hustler*.

Dual Image

Although they did what they could to influence what was said about them in the press, Mary-Kate and Ashley could not control stories that were written about them. In their late teens, a dual image of the sisters began to appear. Sometimes they appeared to be living the wholesome, idealized lifestyle their brand represented, and at other times they appeared to be breaking apart that image. They put out clean movies and issued upbeat words of encouragement to fans through vehicles such their *Teen People* diary, but they also did interviews for stories that were accompanied by seductive, brooding photos that did not seem to be in line with the image they had traditionally represented. For example, they were pictured with a bright and cheery look on the video cover for *The*

Challenge, but posed provocatively in *Vanity Fair* and *Rolling Stone,* where they were called "America's Favorite Fantasy."[32]

The possibility that they would not continue to live up to their wholesome image was seen as a danger to the success of their business. "The twins have done a great job in perpetuating their image together as a pair that's wholesome, spunky, athletic, but as they grow up, they become more independent," noted James Bell, who worked for a brand consulting firm. "The challenge is keeping them as a pair. They could also turn into people you find in the *National Enquirer.*"[33]

People who worked with Mary-Kate and Ashley were extremely supportive of them, however, and gave the impression that they had made it through a busy, prestige-filled childhood and teenage years without any problems. "People are always looking for the dirt on them, but there isn't any," said Elizabeth Kruger, who wrote three films for the Olsens. "They're just normal girls who try to lead a regular teenage life. These two girls have been working since they were little and know the value of hard work. They are very responsible."[34]

Other reports about their activities indicated that the pair sometimes strayed from the straight and narrow path they purported to follow. When they went to a party at a friend's house after a winter dance in early 2004, photos of the event were published in which Mary-Kate was shown near a group of beer bottles. Although she was holding a water bottle, she later admitted that she and Ashley hung around people who drink. "Listen, we're not perfect," Ashley said. "I'm not saying that we drink. I'm not saying that we don't drink. All I'm saying is we're making the right decisions for us."[35]

In addition to mainstream publications, their pictures began to appear in gossipy tabloids. The papers printed stories that hinted at drug use and eating disorders. The girls vehemently denied that they had problems with addiction or eating disorders and insisted that the parties were really just normal gatherings with their friends. They did not want to risk tarnishing the image that had built such a successful company but at the same time were rebellious enough to insist on doing what they wanted with their social lives.

New York Minute

Growing up was proving to be more difficult than it had first appeared it would be. In addition to being trailed by photographers who kept a very attentive eye on their social lives, the girls soon had to deal with criticism of their new movie. Until this time, few of their videos had been extensively reviewed, and they had been shielded from the criticism. Rather than being judged on the girls' acting abilities, their movies' success had been measured by how many copies were sold, how much money they brought in, and whether or not they could keep a young girl's attention. *New York Minute,* on the other hand, was different. It was released in theaters nationwide and was reviewed by critics who decided whether or not video stars Mary-Kate and Ashley could hold their own on the big screen.

Shown here on the set of New York Minute, *Mary-Kate and Ashley took it in stride when the movie bombed at the box office.*

Unfortunately for the twins, the answer was a resounding "no." The movie flopped at the box office and brought in only $6 million in the first weekend, much less than expected for a movie that cost $40 million to make. The movie's choppy style caused reviewer Lisa Schwartzbaum to call it "manufactured mayhem."[36] Although Thorne had said they were aiming to make a mainstream comedy that would appeal to nineteen- and twenty-year-olds, the movie's story line is similar to that of the twins' feature videos. Ashley plays Jane, a serious student, and Mary-Kate has the role of her rebellious sister Roxy, who is not averse to skipping classes. They end up spending a day together romping around New York City as Jane struggles to make it to a prestigious event, where she is due to deliver a speech that could get her into Oxford, and Roxy tries to get to a video shoot. Along the way there are car chases, a makeover, goofy criminals, and, of course, boys. The formula had worked for them numerous times on video but did not translate well to the big screen. "The movie, a travelogue com-

When Mary-Kate and Ashley hosted Saturday Night Live *in May 2004, they played schoolgirls from the 1970s in one skit and paparazzi in another.*

edy in the mold of the Olsen video capers *Passport to Paris* and *When in Rome* has the tone of bland chaos: much movement, no energy," wrote reviewer Richard Corliss. "Having behaved on camera their entire lives, the Olsens know how to counterfeit emotion, though not, yet, how to convey it." [37]

The girls took the criticism in stride, however, and did not seem to mind the blemish on their careers. "They were incredibly mature about it," said Dennie Gordon, the movie's director. "They said, 'Okay, I guess we can't open a movie just yet. Next!'" [38] The pair continued with plans to promote the movie overseas rather than dwelling on its dismal returns in the United States. There would eventually be a silver lining, as the movie made it into the top ten on the video sales chart. When reviewer Nancy Churnin took another look at the movie when it was released on DVD a few months later, she softened a bit. "On the television screen, the jokes seem a little less awful and their less-than-swift delivery a little more endearing," she said. [39]

Not as It Seemed

The stinging criticism of their movie was just one in a series of setbacks for the girls. They sued a video game manufacturer for doing a poor job of putting out a line of games in which they were featured. In mid-May, Mary-Kate had a minor auto accident on a Los Angeles freeway. Although she was not hurt, her Range Rover had to be towed from the scene. Ashley ended her relationship with Matt Kaplen after dating him for more than two years, and rumors of drugs and eating disorders continued to follow the sisters.

They refuted the rumors and even made fun of them when they hosted *Saturday Night Live*. In a sketch that cast the twins as invasive and rude photographers, they shouted, "Mary-Kate, you're so skinny—eat a sandwich!" [40] They were aware of the rumors but denied there was anything wrong. "We don't have problems!" Ashley emphasized. "There's nothing to worry about," Mary-Kate insisted. [41]

A look at their media empire would suggest they were right. They had successfully turned a stint as child actresses into a $1-billion merchandising empire. Their videos had earned $750 million in retail sales, and they had added books, music, fashion, cosmetics, and home accessories to their repertoire. In addition, their names and faces graced a multitude of other products aimed at young girls, from dolls to board games to toothpaste. Yet, as extensive as their brand had become, they had managed their image so carefully that people did not seem to tire of it.

While their business was in great shape, however, the girls themselves were not. The pair graduated from high school in early June 2004 and seemed to be poised to take on their new titles as co-presidents of Dualstar Entertainment when they turned eighteen a week later. However, things did not go as planned. When their birthday arrived, Ashley celebrated alone with friends. Mary-Kate had entered a facility in order to be treated for an eating disorder.

The twins had seemed to have made it through a busy, prestige-filled childhood and teenage years without any major problems. They were responsible girls who tried to lead a life as regular teenagers. However, that did not make them immune to problems that other teens under pressure also face. The challenge of holding up their image and fulfilling the demands of their career, as well as their desire to do well in school, began to weigh on the Olsens as their high school years came to a close. Before they could move on to the next stage of their lives, Mary-Kate had to get a life-threatening disorder under control, and Ashley would be there to help.

Chapter 6

Moving Ahead

$\mathbf{M}$ARY-KATE AND ASHLEY'S lives would be filled with changes after they graduated from high school. They would move from California to New York, trade in high school classes for college courses, and leave their parents' homes for one of their own. They were becoming more independent, but also had struggles to face. Mary-Kate's eating disorder could be fatal if she did not get it under control. With her sister's support and the help of professionals, she would need to examine how she responded to the pressures of school, work, and their growing business. The girls' future looked promising, but their lives would not be without challenges.

Struggling with an Eating Disorder

Sometime during high school, before her senior year began, Mary-Kate had developed an eating disorder. She had always seemed to thrive on the excitement and pressure of the entertainment and fashion businesses, but the addition of schoolwork and planning for college put her under a great deal of pressure. When the pressure began to get out of control, Mary-Kate responded by turning inward. Unable to get rid of the demands that were placed upon her, she looked to manipulate something she did have power over: her eating.

There had been signs that Mary-Kate was not as happy with herself as it seemed on the outside. When she wrote her college admissions essay, at a time when she had the world in front of her, she wrote about a fear of having everything to lose. She seemed to be confident about her looks, but doubts crept into her mind. In a 2003 interview on the CBS show *48 Hours,* she asked Ashley why she was so pretty, while she felt she was ugly. In addition, she

Anorexia

In the summer of 2004 Mary-Kate entered treatment for an eating disorder reported to be anorexia nervosa, a disorder that affects an estimated 1 percent of female adolescents. Anorexics refuse to maintain a normal body weight for their height and age and are intensely afraid of becoming fat, even though they are underweight. Anorexics do not see what their weight loss is doing to their health, as they lose the ability to evaluate themselves objectively. They base how they feel about themselves on their weight. An anorexic person may have feelings of despair, be fearful of not measuring up to others' expectations, and continually try to please everyone.

A person with anorexia uses food to deal with emotional problems. She or he may look for excuses not to eat or may eat only a few types of food. A person with anorexia may also chew food and then spit it out or eat only low-fat foods and drink diet soda. Compulsive exercise can also be part of the disorder, and anorexics may often look critically at themselves in the mirror.

Anorexics risk dying from starvation, and about 6 percent of people with anorexia die from the disorder. The heart and brain may be damaged by anorexia, and bones may become brittle.

Treatment for anorexia often involves more than a year of counseling to resolve the emotional issues that are at the root of the eating problems. Help for people with anorexia is available from the National Association of Anorexia Nervosa and Associated Disorders in Highland Park, Illinois (www.anad.org).

Mary-Kate's backless dress reveals how emaciated she became in 2004 as a result of her eating disorder.

The Olsens review a scene from New York Minute *on a video monitor. Mary-Kate was able to hide her eating disorder during filming.*

was very aware that the stores that sold their clothing and cosmetics also carried the celebrity gossip magazines that were splashed with unflattering photos of her. "Those articles are sold in Wal-Mart, where our fans shop," she said. "Do you know how much responsibility that puts on me for something I didn't do?"[42] Her father had been well aware of the pressure his daughters were under to be role models. "They've been put on such a pedestal–I'd have shaky knees," he said.[43]

Mary-Kate's family had been aware of her problem for some time and had tried to handle it without putting her into treatment. During her senior year in high school, an adult ate with Mary-Kate on most days. Her father told her she could not drive her Range Rover until she started eating. Although these efforts showed their concern, they were not enough.

Mary-Kate had hidden her problem well. The cast and crew of the movie *New York Minute* ate with her and had not suspected that an eating disorder was an issue. "I had a lot of meals with her, and it didn't seem there was anything wrong," Gordon said.[44] *Teen People* reported that she dived into chocolate cake at the buffet table during an early-morning photo shoot. However, when a published photo showed her with extremely thin legs, jutting shoulder blades and a wan face, fans began to suspect that Mary-Kate was unhealthy. The twins had always been small and thin, but now Mary-Kate had taken thinness to the extreme and was steadily getting worse.

In June, shortly before Mary-Kate's eighteenth birthday, her father and her therapist committed her to a treatment facility. As painful as it was for them to make Mary-Kate enter the facility, they could see that she was not getting better on her own and did not want the eighty-six-pound girl to die from not eating. Mary-Kate also realized it was something she had to do and did not object. "This is a challenge that Mary-Kate has made a decision to face," said Michael Pagnotta, her representative. "This is a challenge she will meet." [45]

Standing by Her Sister

The twins had planned to celebrate their eighteenth birthday on June 13 with a trip to Mexico. However, when the day arrived it was only Ashley who celebrated with pals. Shortly afterward, news of Mary-Kate's admission to the treatment center was revealed in the press.

Ashley had considered going on a planned publicity tour of Australia to promote their movie *New York Minute* but decided to stay near her sister instead. She admitted that Mary-Kate had been struggling with the problem for quite a while but said it did not have anything to do with the amount of work Mary-Kate did or the success she had. Rather, the disorder was something that anyone might have to face. "This is an issue that a girl down the street can have," Ashley said. "It's an issue a lot of people deal with." [46]

She visited her sister at the rehab center to offer encouragement. She also gave reports to the media that her sister was doing well. She said that Mary-Kate was taking some needed time for herself and added that she would be there for her whenever Mary-Kate needed her.

At the Center

Mary-Kate spent six weeks at the Cirque Lodge treatment center in Sundance, Utah. The upscale facility was located in a picturesque mountain setting, and the time away from school, home, and business concerns allowed her to stop worrying about life's pressures and concentrate on herself. Mary-Kate stayed in a private room in a luxurious log building and participated in the center's rehab program. She also participated in outdoor sports such as horseback riding and rope climbing, activities that helped her push the limits of what she could do and trust that others would be there to catch her and keep her safe.

The center also offers treatment for drug dependency, but family representatives emphatically denied that Mary-Kate was in rehab for drug use. Her treatment was for an eating disorder, which some said was anorexia. All of her family members came from California to visit her, as did her boyfriend, David Katzenberg, the twenty-one-year-old son of movie producer Jeffrey Katzenberg. They attended some of the group therapy sessions with Mary-Kate. When her treatment period at the center ended, she was escorted home by family members.

Mary-Kate's boyfriend David Katzenberg supported her during treatment for her eating disorder.

Mary-Kate left the center in the middle of the night to avoid scrutiny by the media. Her stay did not last as long as some had expected it would, as several months rather than six weeks is a more standard time frame for the type of treatment she received. However, others said it was also normal to have a shorter inpatient stay followed by treatment outside the facility. Mary-Kate would continue to have an eating coach, who was paid $1,000 a day, attend therapy sessions, and meet with a nutritionist. She was ten pounds heavier when she left the center than she had been when she entered it, but anorexia is not quickly cured. She will likely continue to battle the problem for years. "The reason she went [into treatment] was to take care of herself, and that goal was achieved," said Pagnotta. "But it's the beginning of a process, and it's ongoing." [47]

Fans supported Mary-Kate and even felt closer to her because of the problems she was dealing with. Her publicist received thousands of phone calls from fans and their parents while Mary-Kate was in treatment. The girls had always insisted that they led normal lives and had problems just as other teens did. Her treatment for an eating disorder showed Mary-Kate's fallibility and made her seem more real.

While Mary-Kate's eating disorder was a difficult problem for her, it did not seem to tarnish the Olsen appeal. While the twins were dropped from a Got Milk? ad campaign out of sensitivity to Mary-Kate's eating issues, their dealings with other businesses seemed to continue normally. Their clothing line expanded to include swimwear, and it was announced that the line would appear in stores such as Sears and Kohl's in addition to Wal-Mart. A few months after Mary-Kate left the clinic, even food promotions went on as usual, as the twins promoted McDonald's Happy Meals in France.

After the Center

After leaving the center, Mary-Kate seemed upbeat and healthy to many people, in contrast to the frail, downcast girl who had entered the clinic. She spent the first days away from the center with Ashley at the Hotel Bel-Air, to avoid photographers who had their home staked out. She lay by the pool, went to a movie with Ashley, and had lunch with her dad. In the weeks after she left

Soon after receiving treatment for her eating disorder, Mary-Kate appears in public with Ashley to present an MTV video award.

the center, she relaxed with family and friends and planned for the future.

Ashley had been there to support Mary-Kate at the rehab center, and she was with her again when her sister made her first foray into night life after her stay at the center. In early August, Ashley held her sister's hand and led her to the dance floor at a hotel on Sunset Boulevard in Los Angeles. In late August, they were again together when Mary-Kate made her first appearance at an event. The twins presented an award at the MTV Music Awards in Miami, and they thanked fans for the support they had given the pair since Mary-Kate's eating disorder had been revealed.

Not Your Typical Freshmen

Soon after the MTV awards, the Olsens left California behind for college in New York City. Their publicist insisted that they wanted to have a normal college experience and become just another pair of the city's inhabitants. "New York is already a second home to these girls, not a new frontier," Pagnotta said. "What they're trying to do is blend in as New Yorkers, living a day-to-day normal life, getting coffee at a deli, walking down a street without being bothered." [48]

Mary-Kate and Ashley's freshman year at college consisted of classes and homework, but they were not typical college freshmen. Instead of living in a dorm, they roomed together in a $7-million penthouse that had been created from four separate apartments in Greenwich Village and offered views of both the Statue of Liberty and the Empire State Building. Each twin has her own wing, as there are two master bedrooms with adjoining studies. The five-thousand-square-foot piece of real estate has two guest bedrooms, a screening room, kitchen and breakfast nook, living room, family room, and laundry room.

In addition to their penthouse in New York, the girls also had a new home in California. During the summer they purchased a

Gallatin School of Individualized Study

In 2004 Mary-Kate and Ashley began college at the Gallatin School of Individualized Study, a college within New York University. While the university has about fifty thousand students, the Gallatin School has only about twelve hundred undergraduates. Students in the school have the opportunity to design their own courses of study, and they have concentrations rather than majors. They get credit for classes at New York University, internships, and independent study programs.

Since the girls never had time to take elective classes while they were in high school, Mary-Kate hoped that college would give her the opportunity to explore different subjects that meshed with their interests. She was interested in directing and photography, while Ashley leaned toward psychology. They are not the first celebrities to attend New York University. John F. Kennedy Jr. went to law school there, and actor Alec Baldwin and model Christy Turlington also earned degrees from the college.

home in Bel-Air, which has views of the ocean and city. The home cost $4 million and is a place for them to stay when they return to California during school breaks.

While their purchases appeared extravagant for a pair of college freshmen, their spokesman said their decision to live away from the typical student dorms in New York was done out of consideration for others. They did not want any potential stir they might cause to interfere with other students' education. When they had visited the dorms the previous year while looking at the school, a crowd had quickly gathered around them. In addition, they were routinely followed by a pack of twenty photographers. Living away from the dorms, they felt, gave them the best chance at having some privacy.

Business as Usual

Their New York penthouse also gave the girls the space they needed to take care of their business responsibilities. When they turned eighteen, they gained control of their entertainment company and received access to their multimillion-dollar trust funds. They continued reading scripts and approving fashion designs for their apparel line, in addition to keeping up with their studies.

Mary-Kate and Ashley did not leave their business behind when they moved from one coast to another. Thorne moved into an apartment below theirs, and a design team for mary-kateandashley set up shop in a nearby townhouse. Thorne had plans to take their products worldwide and expand their customer base to adults and boys. He also wanted to see the girls produce movies that tackled tough issues. "They won't star in them, and they'll have more latitude as producers," he said, adding that the films would address "really hard-edge, horrible things that have happened in this country that they want people to know about."[49] He was even looking beyond the girls' college years, and talked about a marriage magazine that would be on the drawing board for the girls when they reached their late twenties.

Reinventing Their Image, Again

The Olsens' college quarters were a microcosm of what they had become: young women who did ordinary things but, as much as they had hated to admit it, did not live ordinary lives. As copresidents of a billion-dollar company, they were each worth $137 million and were tied at number 31 on *Fortune*'s list of the forty richest Americans under forty.

In New York they were no longer concerned with looking frugal. They spent their first weeks there thoroughly enjoying life in the city. They attended fashion shows and the U.S. Open tennis tournament, where they spent more time signing autographs and chatting with people in their box than watching the action on the court. They shopped, visited nightclubs, and stopped in at coffee bars. They toured the elite Hamptons resort area and mingled with J-Lo at an event celebrating the one hundredth anniversary of the Coty fragrance company.

Both were also starting new chapters in their love lives. Ashley had broken up with her steady boyfriend the previous spring, and Mary-Kate broke up with Katzenberg as school started. They began going to clubs and visiting the Hamptons resort area with thirty-year-old club owner Scott Sartiano and his friend Ali Fatourechi, to the delight of tabloid photographers who followed them.

Thorne was not the only person who had discovered that the twins' images helped sell products. The sisters' faces were frequently featured on the cover of celebrity gossip magazines, as the publishers went after an audience who had grown up with the girls and was curious to find out just what they were up to in the big city. The photographers diligently captured Mary-Kate's eating habits and hinted that the girls were living lives that went against their wholesome image.

While they were not about to stay home, however, the girls also wanted to make school a priority. When they were invited to attend a party after the Coty event, Ashley declined, saying they had school the next day. They received numerous requests from reporters and television personalities who wanted to interview them and get Mary-Kate to open up in public about her eating disorder, but the girls refused. For the time being they concentrated on school and used their free time for themselves.

In September 2004, Ashley and Mary-Kate pose with Jennifer Lopez at a star-studded party celebrating the anniversary of Coty fragrance.

Foundation for the Future

Mary-Kate and Ashley continued to work with the entertainment business they had helped build, but college also offered them the opportunity to explore new avenues. They could take elective classes and explore areas they had not had time to study while they were in high school. Their studies would give them a foundation for the future, when they would decide whether to continue to follow the successful mary-kateandashley brand that was already in place or take a chance with new projects.

Tween Competition

Although there had been few other brands aimed at young girls when Mary-Kate and Ashley began selling videos and CDs, by the time they were eighteen they had plenty of competition for "tweens," girls between the ages of eight and fourteen. Younger stars who had made it big on television were testing their talents on the big screen, as well as releasing CDs. While the Olsens still had command of a large share of the money spent by their target audience, there were others aiming for the same dollars.

Tops among their competition were actresses Hilary Duff and Lindsay Lohan. Duff had starred as Lizzie McGuire in television and movie roles, and her first solo album went triple platinum. She espoused a clean image and introduced her own line of accessories available at Target. Actress Lohan had an edgier image than either the Olsens or Duff. She was praised for her acting in hit movies such as *Freaky Friday* and *Mean Girls*, but her penchant for parties and an older boyfriend, Wilmer Valderrama of *That 70s Show*, made her the bad girl of the group.

A host of other young girls was also waiting in the wings. Actress Amanda Bynes was another Nickelodeon star who was making movies, and former Cosby Show Kid Raven-Symone sang and had her own show, *That's So Raven*, on the Disney Channel. Ashlee Simpson, the younger sister of singer Jessica Simpson, had a reality show on MTV, just like her big sister. The singer also had a number 1 album entitled *Autobiography*. In addition, Britney Spears's younger sister, Jamie Lynn, was entertaining audiences on Nickelodeon's *All That* and *Zoe 101*.

With a hit television show, movie roles, and a line of accessories at Target stores, Hilary Duff offers keen competition to the Olsen sisters.

While they were becoming more independent, however, Mary-Kate and Ashley were not yet entirely on their own. Mary-Kate still needed to carefully monitor her eating habits and had an eating coach with her in New York. Thorne continued to run the daily operations of their business in close proximity to the twins. The businesses that had been intertwined with their lives for so long would be part of their college years as well.

Mary-Kate and Ashley did not know a life that had not been mingled with work. As actresses, singers, and the faces behind a multimillion-dollar company, they had made more than thirty videos, released more than a dozen albums, and were the main characters in books and video games. They had their own fashion and merchandise lines built upon their bright, wholesome image. For the most part, they held up well under the pressure of having so many business projects that hinged on their actions. They had proven that they could continue to connect with fans and consumers as they grew. Their next challenge would be to prove the same thing as adults.

Their parents had given them a grounded upbringing and solid values. Thorne had helped them establish a thriving business. They now had more freedom than they had ever known, and it would be up to them to use it wisely.

Notes

Chapter 1: Little Stars

1. Quoted in Damon Romine, *Our Story: Mary-Kate and Ashley Olsen's Official Biography.* New York: HarperEntertainment, 2000, pp. 20–21.
2. Quoted in Emily Ormand, "Double Take," *TV Guide,* December 8, 1990, p. 2.
3. Quoted in Ormand, "Double Take," p. 2.
4. Quoted in Ormand, "Double Take," p. 2.
5. Quoted in Ormand, "Double Take," p. 2.

Chapter 2: Building on Stardom

6. Ken Tucker, "I Am the Cute One," *Entertainment Weekly,* October 1, 1993, p. 71.
7. Quoted in Joe Rhodes, "Tycoon Tykes," *TV Guide,* August 7, 1993, p. 6.

Chapter 3: Growing with Their Fans

8. Quoted in John Lippman, "Double Vision," *Wall Street Journal,* March 10, 1997, p. A1.
9. Quoted in Lippman, "Double Vision," p. A1.
10. Quoted in Lippman, "Double Vision," p. A8.
11. Quoted in Michelle Tauber, "Two Cool," *People Weekly,* May 3, 2004, p. 108.
12. Quoted in Dana Kennedy, "Twin Peaks," *Entertainment Weekly,* May 17, 1996, p. 38.
13. Quoted in Kennedy, "Twin Peaks," p. 38.
14. Quoted in Lippman, "Double Vision," p. A8.
15. Quoted in Lippman, "Double Vision," p. A8.

16. Quoted in Kennedy, "Twin Peaks," p. 38.

17. Quoted in *Entertainment Weekly,* "New Shows (Two of a Kind)," September 11, 1998, p. 84.

18. *People Weekly,* "Two of a Kind," September 21, 1998, p. 27.

19. Quoted in *Entertainment Weekly,* "New Shows (Two of a Kind)," p. 84.

Chapter 4: Becoming a Brand

20. Quoted in David Grainger, "The Human Truman Show," *Fortune,* July 8, 2002, p. 96.

21. Quoted in Mim Udovitch, "The Olsen Juggernaut," *New York Times Magazine,* May 27, 2001, p. 24.

22. Quoted in Grainger, "The Human Truman Show," p. 96.

23. Quoted in "Behind the Scenes" of *Winning London,* DVD, directed by Craig Shapiro. Burbank, CA: Warner Home Video, 2001.

24. Quoted in Romine, *Our Story,* p. 44.

Chapter 5: Juggling It All

25. Quoted in Romine, *Our Story,* p. 32.

26. Quoted in Lauren Brown, "Mary-Kate and Ashley," *CosmoGirl!,* May 2003, p. 136.

27. Quoted in Rebecca Louie, "Twin Tycoons Are Worth $300 Million– and They're Just 17," *New York Daily News,* November 24, 2003.

28. Quoted in Jancee Dunn, "The Sisters of Perpetual Abstinence," *Rolling Stone,* September 4, 2003, p. 88.

29. Quoted in Brown, "Mary-Kate and Ashley," p. 136.

30. Quoted in Brown, "Mary-Kate and Ashley," p. 136.

31. Quoted in Laura Morgan, "Prom Fever," *Teen People,* April 1, 2004, p. 72.

32. Thomas K. Arnold, "Just Call Them the Olsen 'Individuals,'" *USA Today,* April 29, 2004, p. D6.

33. Quoted in Ann D'Innocenzio, "Mary-Kate and Ashley Expand a $1 Billion Brand," Associated Press, June 22, 2002.

34. Quoted in Louie, "Twin Tycoons Are Worth $300 Million."

35. Quoted in Tauber, "Two Cool," p. 108.

36. Lisa Schwartzbaum, "New York Minute: The Sad Truth: Kids'll Keep This Film Around Longer than the Title," *Entertainment Weekly,* May 14, 2004, p. 48.

37. Richard Corliss, "Olsens in Bid to Buy Disney: Actually, No. But at 17, the TV Twins Are Powerful, Rich, and the Stars of Their Very Own, Very Bad Movie," *Time,* May 17, 2004, p. 78.

38. Quoted in Michelle Tauber et al., "Mary-Kate's Private Battle," *People Weekly,* July 5, 2004, p. 54.

39. Nancy Churnin, "New York Minute Might Be Worth a Second Look," *Dallas Morning News,* August 24, 2004.

40. Quoted in Tauber et al., "Mary Kate's Private Battle," p. 54.

41. Quoted in Tauber, "Two Cool," p. 108.

Chapter 6: Moving Ahead

42. Quoted in Tauber, "Two Cool," p. 108.

43. Quoted in Tauber, "Two Cool," p. 108.

44. Quoted in Tauber et al., "Mary-Kate's Private Battle," p. 54.

45. Quoted in Tauber et al., "Mary-Kate's Private Battle," p. 54.

46. Quoted in Greg Adkins et al., "Sister to Sister," *People Weekly,* July 12, 2004, p. 19.

47. Quoted in Mike Lipton, "What's Next for Mary-Kate?" *People Weekly,* August 9, 2004, p. 60.

48. Quoted in Geraldine Baum, "Olsen Twins at NYU but in a Class of Their Own," *Los Angeles Times,* September 16, 2004. www.contra costatimes.com.

49. Quoted in Dunn, "The Sisters of Perpetual Abstinence," p. 88.

Important Dates in the Lives of Mary-Kate and Ashley Olsen

1986

Mary-Kate and Ashley are born on June 13 in Sherman Oaks, California.

1987

The twins capture the role of Michelle on television's *Full House* and begin their acting careers.

1990

The twins' *Full House* character, Michelle, is featured in a book series aimed at young girls.

1991

Entertainment lawyer Robert Thorne becomes the girls' new manager. A talking Michelle doll is released.

1992

Mary-Kate and Ashley star in their first movie, *To Grandmother's House We Go,* and each has her own role. Their first recording, *Brother for Sale,* released in October.

1993

Thorne creates the Dualstar Entertainment Group to produce the girls' movies, music, and other ventures and makes Mary-Kate and Ashley executive producers. Their second album, *I Am the Cute One,* is released, and the girls sing from their first two albums on *Our First Video.* They also make their second movie, *Double, Double, Toil and Trouble,* which is produced by Dualstar.

1994

Mary-Kate and Ashley make an appearance in the movie *The Little Rascals* and make their third feature film for television, *How the West Was Fun*. They begin a series of mystery videos, portraying the Trenchcoat Twins in *The Adventures of Mary-Kate and Ashley: The Case of the Thorn Mansion* and *The Case of the Logical I Ranch*.

1995

The final episode of *Full House* airs in August. The girls hit the big screen with *It Takes Two* and release the first video in the *You're Invited* series, which showcases them having a sleepover. They add four titles to the mystery series as well.

1996

The girls continue to release videos in their *Adventures* and *You're Invited* series.

1997

The final video in the *Adventures* series, *The Case of the Volcano Mystery,* is released, as are four videos in the *You're Invited* series.

1998

The girls return to television with the series *Two of a Kind,* which is canceled after one season, and make their first feature-length video, *Billboard Dad*.

1999

The girls make *Switching Goals,* a sports movie. *Passport to Paris* becomes the first in a series of movies that take the twins to locations around the world.

2000

Mary-Kate and Ashley travel to Australia to make *Our Lips Are Sealed* and also release the last of the videos in the *You're Invited* series, which focuses on a school dance.

2001

London and the Bahamas are the settings for their next movies, *Winning London* and *Holiday in the Sun*. They begin work on a new television series, *So Little Time,* and the animated *Mary-Kate and Ashley in Action!*

2002

The girls turn sixteen and let fans in on the celebration with the movie *Getting There: Sweet 16 and Licensed to Drive.* The movie *When in Rome* is also released.

2003

The Challenge becomes the final direct-to-video movie for the pair. They also make an appearance in *Charlie's Angels: Full Throttle.*

2004

The twins' first theatrical release in almost a decade, *New York Minute,* does poorly at the box office but rebounds on video. Mary-Kate and Ashley graduate from high school and become copresidents of their production company, Dualstar, when they turn eighteen. Shortly before her eighteenth birthday, Mary-Kate enters a facility where she is treated for an eating disorder. After spending six weeks at the center, she and Ashley move to New York where they begin college at New York University's Gallatin School of Individualized Study.

For Further Reading

Books

Pauline Preiss, *The New Adventures of Mary-Kate and Ashley: The Case of the Logical I Ranch*. New York: HarperEntertainment, 2001. This reprint of one of the first books in the girls' mystery series has the girls looking for a dragon on a dude ranch.

Damon Romine, *Our Story: Mary-Kate and Ashley Olsen's Official Biography*. New York: HarperEntertainment, 2000. An upbeat, sugary look at the Olsens' career, filled with quotes, anecdotes, and photos.

Bailey J. Russell, *Mary-Kate and Ashley Olsen*. Edina, MN: Abdo Publishing, 2004. An easy-to-read biography of the twins.

Kathleen Tracy, *Mary Kate and Ashley Olsen*. Bear, DE: Mitchell Lane Publishers, 2004. A brief biography looking at how the twins have grown in their career.

Periodicals

Jancee Dunn, "The Sisters of Perpetual Abstinence," *Rolling Stone,* September 4, 2003. A look at how the twins are handling growing up.

John Lippman, "Double Vision," *Wall Street Journal,* March 10, 1997. An early look at the Olsens' marketing empire.

Jennifer Wulff, "Pressure to Be Perfect," *People Weekly,* July 26, 2004. In light of Mary-Kate's battle with an eating disorder, the issue of eating disorders among young girls is examined.

Web Sites

mary-kateandashley.com (www.mary-kateandashley.com).
Offers fans a chance to see Mary-Kate and Ashley's latest fashions and products.

People (www.people.com). The online home of *People* magazine provides the latest information on Mary-Kate and Ashley and other celebrities.

TV Tome (www.tvtome.com). Under a search for *Full House,* readers will find a synopsis of each of the show's episodes, as well as goofs that were made in the shows.

Works Consulted

Periodicals

Greg Adkins et al., "Mary-Kate Steps Out," *People Weekly,* August 16, 2004, p. 21.

Greg Adkins et al., "New York, New Men," *People Weekly,* September 20, 2004, p. 21.

Greg Adkins et al., "The Olsen Twins: College Bound," *People Weekly,* December 29, 2003, p. 22.

Greg Adkins et al., "Sister to Sister," *People Weekly,* July 12, 2004, p. 19.

Thomas K. Arnold, "Just Call Them the Olsen 'Individuals,'" *USA Today,* April 29, 2004, p. D6.

Carrie Bell, "Our Senior Year," *Teen People,* October 1, 2003, p. 82.

Lauren Brown, "Mary-Kate and Ashley," *CosmoGirl!,* May 2003, p. 136.

Nancy Churnin, "New York Minute Might Be Worth a Second Look," *Dallas Morning News,* August 24, 2004.

Richard Corliss, "Olsens in Bid to Buy Disney: Actually, No. But at 17, the TV Twins Are Powerful, Rich and the Stars of Their Very Own, Very Bad Movie," *Time,* May 17, 2004, p. 78.

Ann D'Innocenzio, "Mary-Kate and Ashley Expand a $1 Billion Brand," Associated Press, June 22, 2002.

Entertainment Weekly, "New Shows (Two of a Kind)," September 11, 1998, p. 84.

Nicholas Fonseca, "Olsen Twins, Activate!" *Entertainment Weekly,* April 18, 2003, p. 7.

Seth Goldstein, "Time Warner Units Pair Up on Twin Promotion," *Billboard,* July 29, 1995, p. 62.

David Grainger, "The Human Truman Show," *Fortune,* July 8, 2002, p. 96.

Dana Kennedy, "Twin Peaks," *Entertainment Weekly,* May 17, 1996, p. 38.

John Lippman, "Double Vision," *Wall Street Journal,* March 10, 1997.

Mike Lipton, "What's Next for Mary-Kate?" *People Weekly,* August 9, 2004, p. 60.

Rebecca Louie, "Twin Tycoons Are Worth $300 Million–and They're Just 17," *New York Daily News,* November 24, 2003.

Laura Morgan, "Prom Fever," *Teen People,* April 1, 2004, p. 72.

Emily Ormand, "Double Take," *TV Guide,* December 8, 1990, p. 2.

People Weekly, "Two of a Kind," September 21, 1998, p. 27.

Carolyn Ramsay, "The Olsens Inc." *Los Angeles Times,* January 30, 2000.

Joe Rhodes, "Tycoon Tykes," *TV Guide,* August 7, 1993, p. 6.

Lisa Schwartzbaum, "New York Minute: The Sad Truth: Kids'll Keep This Film Around Longer than the Title," *Entertainment Weekly,* May 14, 2004, p. 48.

Michelle Tauber, "Two Cool," *People Weekly,* May 3, 2004, p. 108.

Michelle Tauber et al., "Mary-Kate's Private Battle," *People Weekly,* July 5, 2004, p. 54.

Teen People, "Behind the Scenes: Cover Shoot Scoop," June 1, 2004, p. 50.

Time for Kids, "TFK Q & A," October 23, 1998, p. 8.

Ken Tucker, "I Am the Cute One," *Entertainment Weekly,* October 1, 1993, p. 71.

Mim Udovitch, "The Olsen Juggernaut," *New York Times Magazine,* May 27, 2001, p. 24.

Rebecca Winters, "What the Girls Want," *Time,* April 19, 2004, p. 103.

Ting Yu et al. "Pop Quiz with the Olsen Twins," *People Weekly,* July 1, 2002, p. 22.

Movies

The Adventures of Mary-Kate and Ashley: The Case of the Volcano Mystery, VHS, directed by Michael Krutzan. Burbank, CA: KidVision, 1997.

Billboard Dad, DVD, directed by Alan Metter. Burbank, CA: Warner Home Video, 1998.

The Challenge, DVD, directed by Craig Shapiro. Burbank, CA: Warner Home Video, 2003.

Getting There, VHS, directed by Steve Purcell. Burbank, CA: Buena Vista Home Entertainment, 2002.

New York Minute, VHS, directed by Dennie Gordon. Burbank, CA: Warner Home Video, 2004.

Our Lips Are Sealed, VHS, directed by Craig Shapiro. Burbank, CA: Warner Home Video, 2000.

Switching Goals, VHS, directed by David Steinberg. Burbank, CA: Warner Home Video, 1999.

To Grandmother's House We Go, VHS, directed by Jeff Franklin. Burbank, CA: Warner Brothers Family Entertainment, 1997.

You're Invited to Mary-Kate and Ashley's School Dance Party, DVD, directed by Brad Pratt. Burbank, CA: Warner Home Video, 2003.

When in Rome, DVD, directed by Steve Purcell. Burbank, CA: Warner Home Video, 2002.

Winning London, DVD, directed by Craig Shapiro. Burbank, CA: Warner Home Video, 2001.

Internet Sources

Geraldine Baum, "Olsen Twins at NYU but in a Class of Their Own," *Los Angeles Times,* September 16, 2004. www.contracostatimes. com/mld/cctimes/9678233.htm?1c.

Lia Haberman, "Mary-Kate Deals with 'Health Issue,'" *E! Online News,* June 22, 2004. www.eonline.com/News/Items/0,1,14152,00.html.

Lia Haberman, "Mary-Kate's Fender Bender," *E! Online News,* May 20, 2004. www.eonline.com/News/Items/0,1,14363,00.html.

Internet Movie Database, "Ashley Olsen." www.imdb.com/name/ nm0001580.

Internet Movie Database, "Mary-Kate Olsen." www.imdb.com/name/0001581.

Joel Ryan, "Mary-Kate, Ashley Get Schooled," *E! Online News,* September 7, 2004. www.eonline.com/News/Items/0,1,1,48 80,00.html?news.

Karen Thomas, "School Splits Up Mary-Kate, Beau," *USA Today,* September 8, 2004. www.usatoday.com/life/people/2004-09-08-olsen-breakup_x.htm.

You're Invited to Mary-Kate & Ashley's, "Meet Mary-Kate and Ashley," www.youre-invited.warnerbros.com/cmp/meet.htm.

Sydney Morning Herald, "Tween Queens Call the Shots," September 12, 2004. www.smh.com.au/articles/2004/09/11/1094789739 683.html.

Index

Picture Credits

About the Author

Terri Dougherty writes nonfiction books for children as well as magazine and newspaper articles. A native of Black Creek, Wisconsin, Terri graduated from the University of Wisconsin–Oshkosh and was a newspaper reporter and editor before beginning her freelance writing career. She and husband, Denis, along with their children, Kyle, Rachel, and Emily, have watched many videos starring Mary-Kate and Ashley Olsen and often end their day by watching an episode of *Full House* together.